MINISTERIAL ETHICS, 2ND EDITION

Place order from:

REV. DR. OGBA ONYEIJE
B.Sc, Dip. Th., BA, MA, MA, Ph.D
Tel.: 0803 434 9741

Published in Nigeria by:
DONIL PUBLICATIONS LTD., ABA.

ISBN: 978-978-51522-2-7

Design & Printed by:
DONIL PRINTS LTD.
#4 Ibo Road/4B Ngwa Rd., Aba - Abia State
08036816630, 08066626771, 08020116060

DEDICATION

This book is dedicated to all church leaders-living and dead who are epitomes of ministerial integrity and sanctity.

ACKNOWLEDGMENT

I am grateful to God for his grace and enablement in writing this book. I thank all the authors whose works I consulted.

CONTENTS

PREFACE

God, the creator of man and the universe, is God of principles and a lawgiver. In his character and dealings with man, he operates by the principles and laws he has given. The world and the whole universe operate by the natural laws of the Great Law Giver.
In consonance with God, different professions have their own code of conduct, otherwise called professional ethics, which all their members are committed to in carrying out their professional duties. Hence, there is medical ethics, legal ethics, business ethics, and ministerial ethics, to mention but a few. The importance of professional ethics cannot be overemphasised. So also is the importance of ministerial ethics for church leaders and workers.

There is a dire need for a manual on ministerial ethics to serve as a guide to church leaders and workers so that their services will be acceptable to God and be a blessing to humanity and to the church where they serve. The dearth of written works on the subject of ministerial ethics informed the writing of this book. It serves as a manual for church leaders and workers. It also serves as resource material for teachers of ministerial ethics in theological institutions.

Ogba Onyeije, Ph.D., JP.

FOREWORD

This book, *Ministerial Ethics,* has six chapters that are organically structured and developed to help ministers of the gospel appreciate a decent life. It is a book that calls ministers of the gospel to order in their dealings with their fellow colleagues and the flock of God.

Chapter one discusses the *nature* and *mission* of the church. The nature of the church is known as the body of called-out people of God to proclaim the Gospel of Jesus Christ and gather believers into local churches where they could be built up in the faith and be made effective in the service of God.

Ministerial ethics, which is also known as moral theology or principles of determining what is right and wrong for ministers of the gospel, is the focus of this work. Dr. Onyeije, in *chapter two,* handles this work competently by outlining several bases for demanding conformity to church ministerial ethics. These include professional, theistic, missiological, ecclesiological, anthropological, and biblical basis.

Chapter three examines some ethical theories and the ministry of the church. Some of these theories include emotivism, cultural relativism, utilitarianism, Machiavelism, antinomianism, hedonism, and situationism. Ministers of God and other leaders in the church should not depend on their personal convictions alone in handling issues that come up in the church. The word of God should always serve as the major source of standard to determine ethical issues.

Chapter four ex-rays ethical codes of conducts for those who serve God in various capacities. The author emphasizes the need for hard work, excellence, regularity and punctuality, integrity, loyalty, commitment to servant leadership, discipline, humility, prudent financial management and accountability.

Unethical ministerial conduct is the subject of *chapter five*. Here, the author enumerates some of the conducts that do not befit church leaders. They include different forms of abuse, destructive criticisms, wrong communication patterns, defamation of character, rebelliousness, riots and strikes, campaigns, trespass, betrayal, and other miscellaneous unethical conduct.

Chapter six of this book looks into some socioethical issues in the church. In the study of ethics, this chapter falls in the area of applied ethics. The aspects covered include abortion, euthanasia, assisted suicide, gay marriage, divorce, and remarriage. The author exposes his readers to various aspects of ethical issues that relate to leaders at all levels in the church.

Chapter Seven, which is added in this second edition, deals with ministerial etiquette, protocol, and courtesy. It deals with respect and orderliness in ministerial duties, which ensure peaceful and harmonious relationships in ministry.

The book, *Ministerial Ethics,* is a *must-read* for all leaders in the church. This is a book every minister of the gospel needs. It is diligently written and stands out as one text that all church leaders, including elites, need in order to get correct guides in ministerial activities. I therefore recommend this book to ministers of God at all levels and those under training in various theological institutions and public libraries. Read this book and be informed and especially blessed!

C. C. Okereke
(Professor of Ethics and Sociology of Religion)
Department of Religious Studies & Philosophy Abia State University, Uturu.

CHAPTER 1

THE CHURCH: IT'S NATURE AND MISSION

1.1 The Nature of the Church:

Before delving into the mission of the church, it is pertinent that we understand the nature of the church. According to Reginal M. McDonough, the New Testament word for the Church is "Ekklesia," which translates the Hebrew term "Qahal," which referred to the nation of Israel assembled before God under divine rule (Deut. 31:30). "Ekkaleo," which is the root of "Ekklesia," means "the called-out ones." From the above view of McDonough, it is understandable that the church is the body of the called-out people of God who represent him in the world. The Church is therefore a divine institution that originated in the mind of God and was created to serve him.

M. Uka (1959:9) concurring with the above view on the nature of the Church says: *The Church is a communion of saints; a communion sanctorum. That is, the Church is the called-out people of God who constitute the holy presence of Christ in the world. Its most fundamental task is to build communities of holy character.*

Hunter (1973:53) maintains that the Holy Scripture reflects a dynamic organism called the Church, which is alive and having relationship with the living God and the Resurrected Christ. In his own view on the nature of the Church, Emeka (2011:40) maintains that the evangelicals see the Church as an organism and also an organization. As an organism, it is the body of Christ, of which Christ is the head. The church derives its life from Christ. In the Old and New Testaments, the church is presented as an organism and as an organization. In the views of Gangel (1981:23,24), there are four common uses of the word church: building, denominations, universal church, and local church. Of these four concepts of the church, only the last two—the universal church and the local church are biblical.

Gangel succinctly puts his ideas thus:

> *The Greek word used to designate either universal or local church in the New Testament is the word 'ecclesia'. To the Greeks, the word indicated an assembly of free citizens; however, to the Jews, it would have more theocratic connotations. In the New Testament, the word has three basic uses: (1) A political assembly of free citizens (Acts 19:32) (2) Jewish assembly of the Old Testament (the church in the wilderness) (Acts 7:38) (3). The Christian church: Almost all the New Testament passages, excluding the two mentioned above, deal with the Christian church in either its universal or local form. Because of the extreme importance of this concept, one cannot properly perceive the doctrine of the church without a thorough understanding of the two uses of the word ecclesia. The universal church contains only true believers, whereas the local church may include professing Christians who have not had an experience of regeneration.*

Summarily, the church is the body of the called-out people of God who represent Christ in the world and have a relationship with him as the head. The church may be a local church or the universal church of the born-again whose names are written in heaven.

1.2 The Mission of the Church:

The concern of this segment is on the reason or purpose the Church exist in the world? This consideration is important as it will determine the ethical requirements of church ministry. The code of conduct of any profession is determined by the mission of that profession. Understanding the mission of the church will help to understand and formulate the ethics of church ministry. Many scholars have maintained that the church is not only in the world to evangelize the world through gospel proclamation but also to better the world through socio-economic and political involvements.

Lending credence to the fact that the mission of the Church is not only evangelising but also to serve the world in social ministries as Jesus did, Scott (1973:23) succinctly puts his arguments thus:

> *I now see more clearly that not only the consequences of the commission but the actual commission itself must be understood to include social as well as evangelistic responsibility unless we are to be guilty of distorting the words of Jesus.*

The summary of John Scott's view is that the mission of the church is to evangelise the world with the gospel and to meet the needs of the world through social ministries. The author wholly buys Scott's view. It is very relevant to his work as it is an eye opener to some members and leaders of the Church who do not know that the Church is called of God to meet both the spiritual and the social needs of the world. Griffiths (1980) sees the duty of the Christian mission as planting new churches and perfecting them by making a holistic impact upon the city. He buttresses his argument by citing the Lausanne Covenant Statement on a Christian's social responsibility to the world. An excerpt of the covenant says, "Here too we express penitence both for our neglect and for having sometimes regarded evangelism and social concern as mutually exclusive." Yri (1978:269), in his work, more vividly cites the affirmations of the International Congress on World Evangelisation in its Lausanne Covenant, thus:

> *We affirm that God is both the creator and the judge of all men. We should therefore share his concern for justice and reconciliation throughout human society and for the liberation of men from every kind of oppression. We affirm that evangelism and sociopolitical involvement are both part of our Christian responsibility.*

The World Council of Churches is not silent on the mission of the church to the contemporary world. According to Yri, the World Council of Churches, in its congress on the church's worldwide mission held on April 9-16, 1966, at Wheaton, resolved to "urge all Evangelicals to stand openly and firmly for racial equality, human freedom, and justice throughout the world.

Scarle (1982), writing on "Development Work Fits the Great Commission," maintains that community development is a more effective means of both sharing the gospel of Christ and of relieving suffering. He defines community development as the process of enabling people to identify and attempt to solve their own problems. Howard believes that when Christians actively demonstrate Christ's love by responding to physical need, relationships of trust develop, which often leads to opportunities for sharing Christ's message on a one-to-one basis. He sees a symbiotic relationship between the Church and community development in the sense that not only the Christian community undertakes community development, but that community development increases and strengthens the Church. Furthermore, he maintains that when a local church is lacking in community health, community development is often effective in establishing one.

Howard concludes his discourse by pointing out that the Great Commission and community development are not opposed to each other. Rather, the Christian who patiently and gently helps people learn to relieve their suffering heightens receptivity to the message. People will see Christianity as a vital faith lived out through love and deed. This will help in attracting people to the Christian faith.

Howard's article helps us to understand the need for community development as an aspect of social action of the church in its missionary enterprise to the world. Furthermore, it reveals the symbiotic relationship between social action and church growth.

Hesselgrave (1980), in his own contribution to the subject, examines the heart of the Christian mission and its relationship with social action. He begins his discourse by enumerating the different concepts and different schools of thought concerning the church. According to him, the communists view the church as a chain anchoring the proletariat to the past. The secularists think of the church as an organ without which the individual and society could function just as effectively or even more so.

The liberals see the church as fulfilling its purpose when it permeates society and loses its separate identity. Conservative Christians see the church as being at the heart of the divine purpose, with growth as one of its major responsibilities. Hesselgrave summarises his view of the mission of the Church thus:

The primary mission of the church and therefore of the Christian is to proclaim the gospel of Jesus Christ and gather believers into local churches where they can be built up in the faith and made effective in service, thereby planting new congregations throughout the world (1980:5). He further maintains that the Church has other (secondary) tasks to perform in the world. For instance, he observes that the establishment of hospitals, leprosy settlements, literacy campaigns, and many other humanitarian services have accompanied the progress of Christianity across the face of the earth. Finally, Hesselgrave laments that it is unfortunate that Christian social actions and witnesses seem to be competing and conflicting concerns in Christian outreach when both are biblical and complementary.

Hesselgrave's work is very relevant, as it has made it clear that gospel proclamation and social service are both biblical and should be complementary to each other.

Robb (1989) in his write-up on “The Spiritual Nature of Social Problems,” maintains that there is disagreement among Christians over the question of the most effective way of

transforming the world. The question here is, “Is it through verbal proclamation of the gospel or through social action that is the most effective means of changing our world?” In Robb's own view, the two cannot be separated. In his own words, “Without both, there is simply no good news." According to him, since the Garden of Eden, human beings have gained control over other individuals and whole societies by cooperating with Satan and his evil spirits. Consequently, this has led to wide-scale famine, disease, poverty, slavery, injustice, and suffering. As Christians seek to help the poor and stand against injustice, they are fighting against principalities and powers.

The author accepts Robb's view as it tries despiritualising salvation, thereby making it holistic. The salvation offered by the Kingdom of God as proclaimed by Christ was manifested spiritually, physically, socially, and economically. This made Christ's ministry holistic.

Wagner (1983) examines the social problems of the world and the role of the Church in alleviating them as part of its missionary enterprise. He observes that as much as the final solution to man's material and social problems caused by sin is eschatological. God encourages Christians to do their best in alleviating human problems. According to Wagner, it is this aspect of our Christian responsibility that Glaser, the notable theologian of missions, called "cultural mandate." He opines that the Church, in its mission, has cultural as well as evangelistic duties to fulfill. He calls those who concentrate on the cultural mandate so that they end up neglecting the evangelistic mandate horizontalist and their belief in horizontalism. In his critical look at the relationship between the cultural and evangelistic mandates, Wagner points out five schools of thought and their evangelical positions thus:

A. Those who believe only in the evangelistic mandate.
B. Those who believe only in the cultural mandate.
C. Those that prioritize the cultural mandate.
D. Those that prioritize the evangelistic mandate.
E. Those that consider cultural and evangelistic mandates as equal components of mission.

Wagner sees the first two positions, "A" and "B" as extreme views that should be avoided by biblical Christians. He believes that position "D" is the most consistent of the teaching of the Bible because, according to him while the Church tries to fulfil both mandates, the evangelistic mandate is primary. According to Wagner, while "Radical Disciples" hold to the "E" position, which they call "Holistic Evangelism," liberal Christians hold to the "C" position, which is the theological line that comes out of Geneva.

Headquarters of the World Council of Churches.

In his support for social action as part of Christians' mission in the world, Wagner maintains that as the citizens of the Kingdom of God, we should do all we can to feed the poor, to heal the sick, to comfort the brokenhearted, to liberate the oppressed, and to spread peace upon the earth, for this is not optional. He sees all that the Church can do through social ministry as temporal, penultimate, and stopgap. The author holds the same view as Wagner. The Church should be involved in alleviating human suffering, as Jesus was.

In his support for the evangelistic mandate taking prominent position over social action, Wagner (48) agrees with Winchell, who says:

> *A truly biblical response to social need recognizes that if all who are poor were compensated, if all who are suffering were alleviated, if all who are ignorant were educated, if all who are oppressed were liberated, if all who are hungry were satiated, if all who are deprived were elevated, the world might become a near perfect place. But without the life transforming power of the gospel, sin would soon be revealed, and the cycle of poverty, suffering, oppression, ignorance, hunger, and deprivation would soon be repeated.*

Wagner (1971) in his book: *Your Church Can Grow,* examines the Church's involvement in social service and social action. He maintains that the second sub-priority in doing Christ's work in the world is social involvement. He cites Jesus as an example of an ideal missionary who was socially involved in his ministry. Jesus healed the sick, fed the hungry, cast out demons, and identified with the poor and the outcast as part of his missionary work. Wagner goes further to dichotomise social service from social action. According to him, social service is designed to relieve immediate human needs: healing the sick, feeding the hungry, etc., while social action makes a radical demand to change the structure of society so that the poor and the oppressed can get a fair piece of the social pie, so to speak. This work combines the two concepts under the term "social action." It is the author's opinion that members of the Church should be involved in rendering social service as well as changing unjust social structures to bring to an end inequality, oppression, and injustice.

McGravan (1990) maintains that it is not expected of missionary agencies that proceed from one country to another to engage in social action that will engender rebellions among the masses and thus help them to achieve political, economic, and cultural goals. With the Church, the case is different. Since Church is made of citizens of the country who are part and parcel of the oppressed and the oppressors, it cannot avoid the ceaseless struggle going on between the classes and the masses. He concludes that when Churches multiply in a non-Christian population, they will bring God's purposes for his children to bear on the particular part of the social order that they can influence.

McGavran's work is valuable to this work. It has given us an insight that in any missionary field, it is not expected of foreign missionary agencies to engage in radical social action that will disrupt the existing social order. Such action is left for the established Churches made up of the citizens of the country who are part and parcel of the oppressors and the oppressed. In its missionary enterprise, the church should therefore be involved in programs that still transform the communities socially, politically, economically, and culturally.

Ezigbo (1996), in his own contribution on the mission of the Church observes that there are erroneous views harboured today by both the clergy and the laity regarding the mission of the Church. According to him, some think that the duty the Church has is just to register its presence in the world by magnificent buildings.

Another group thinks that the Church is meant to be “a mansion," a fortified human kingdom that is callous to the cry of the world. The third group of people are those who see the Church as a welfare institution. In his conclusion, he points out that these views are wrong and maintains that “the Church is not meant to be a “mansion” but a "mission,” and the mission of the Church is missions and evangelism.

Steam (1991:42) maintains that the Church is not called to choose either evangelism or social action. It is rather called to balance the two.

In the book, *Special Needs, Special Ministry,* Tada (2004) discusses the need for the Churches to be involved in social ministries, especially for children with special needs because of their disabilities. He describes special needs as disabilities that prevent children from progressing mentally, physically, and emotionally at the cultural pace. He enumerates the disabilities as including hyperactivity with short attention spans, distractibility and impulsiveness, poor visual/motor skills and poor large muscles and fine motor coordination, rapid and excessive changing of mood and reasoning, faulty perception with a repetition of thought or action, problems with social interaction, and inconsistent and unpredictable behaviour.

The author points out that Jesus Christ had a big heart for those with special needs in his missionary work in these words:

> *There is nothing in how Jesus responded to people with disabilities that indicates that he respected them any less than the healthy crowds that surrounded him. Reading through the gospel, it is easy to see that Jesus didn't turn away the disabled, ridiculed them, or suggested they were incapable of discipleship or service. He welcomed and healed the sickest of the sick and, likely, the most disfigured lepers. He gave undivided attention to the deafmute, then he touched and healed him (Matthew 8:1-4).*

The author calls on all Christian denominations to emulate Christ as our example and be involved in special need ministries for the disabled. He sees special ministry for the disabled as a necessity for carrying out the Great Commission handed down to the Church by the Lord Jesus.

Tada's work is very informative and relevant to this work as it has highlighted the fact that the Church is not only expected to be committed to social action, it is also expected to go as far as designing special ministry for those who are physically challenged. In the author's opinion, Tada's list of those with special needs because of disability should expressly include the blind, the deaf, and the cripple. Such inclusion will make the list more embracing.

From the opinion of these contributors, we can conclude this chapter by saying that the mission of the Church is to evangelize the world by proclaiming the gospel as well as meeting the social needs of suffering humanity as Jesus did.

The nature and mission of the church make it very necessary to have church ministerial ethics that do not compromise the nature of the church or sabotage its mission to the world. This will make the church and its ministry relevant and acceptable to the people of the world wherever the gospel is preached.

CHAPTER 2

CONFORMITY TO CHURCH MINISTERIAL ETHICS

2.1 Definition of Ethics:

Ethics has been defined in different ways by different scholars. Agha (2010:1) defines it as "a normative science which sees man as a moral agent and considers his actions, habits, and character with a view to ascertaining their rightness or wrongness". He analyzed Ethics as dealing with:

a. What man should desire and what he should avoid.
b. What man ought or ought not to do.
c. What moral power is necessary to attain the end and accomplish duty?

The above three points can be summarized in three words: values, duties, and virtues.

Norman J. Bulls sees Ethics as the science of human conduct; the pursuit of good life. In the opinions of Geisler and Feinberg (1980:353), Ethics is the study of what is right and what is wrong in human behavior.

Ethics is that branch of philosophy that deals with the rightness or wrongness of human, conduct, and the ought and ought not of life! It examines man's values, behaviours, duties, virtues, and motives to ascertain their rightness or wrongness.

Church ministerial Ethics based on the above definitions of ethics is after the following:

a. Having the right desire (value system) in doing Church work.
b. Carrying out the duties we are expected to carry out as Church leaders and workers in line with the mission of the Church.
c. Having the right motive in doing God's work.
d. Having the right virtue in Church leadership and business.

e. Abiding by the code of conduct and principles that guide Church business.

In his explanation of and the meaning of ethics, Okereke (2012:103) maintains:

> *Ethics which is a major branch of philosophy encompasses right conduct and a good life. It is significantly broader than the common conception of analyzing right and wrong. A central aspect of ethics is "the good life", the life worth living or life that is simply satisfying, which is held by many philosophers to be more important than traditional moral conduct.*

From the above, it is vividly clear that ethics is all about the right and wrong conduct of man in relation to fellow man and to God. It is with this understanding that ministerial ethics is treated in this book.

2.2 Basis for Demanding Conformity to Church Ministerial Ethics

In every demand of God from man, there are bases; just as there are bases for demanding conformity to ministerial ethics. The basis for demanding conformity to ministerial ethics is discussed under the headings below.

a. Professional Basis: All professions have their professional ethics otherwise called code of conduct. Non-conformity with professional ethics leads to withdrawal of license. If a lawyer violates legal professional ethics, he is debarred. If a doctor violates medical professional ethics, he is deregistered. The same thing happens in every other profession. Thus, in every profession, there is an insistence on compliance with professional ethics.

If in the secular world, professional ethics is insisted on being complied with, more is expected in church ministry. The ministers, workers, and leaders of the church should be epitomes of ministerial ethics and thus show examples to different professionals. At this juncture, one may ask: Is church ministry a profession to demand a code of conduct for which professions are known? In other words, can a gospel minister be considered a professional to the extent that they are expected to adhere to ethical standards?

At this juncture, it is pertinent to look at the definition of a professional. The Oxford Advanced Learner's Dictionary defines a professional as a person "having a job that needs special training and a high level of education". It defines a profession as "a type of job that needs special training or skill especially one that needs a high level of education".

Sociologists who have written about the nature of professions and professionals have developed two schools of thought: The Harvard School led by Talcott Parsons and the Chicago School represented by Eliot Fredson. The Harvard School which is functionalist in approach sees a profession as "a distinct occupation characterized by complex knowledge, social importance and high degree of responsibility". The Chicago school sees a professional as a *"semi-mythic construct"* created by members of an occupation to obtain social and economic advantage (Joe E. Trull and James E. Carter, 2004:30).
Using the functionalist idea, James Adams (1958:156) gives the following characteristics of a profession:

1. It performs a unique and essential social service
2. It requires a long period of general and specialized training, usually in connection with a university.
3. It presupposes skills that are subjected to rational analysis.
4. Service to the community rather than economic gain is supposed to be the dominant motive
5. Standards of competence are defined by a comprehensive self-governing organization of practitioners.
6. A high degree of autonomy.

7. Some code of ethics

From the information garnered above, the author's opinion is that an ideal minister of the gospel is a professional and is more than a professional.

James Glasse (1968:13) urging Church leaders to reaffirm their vocational identity as professionals, suggests that the religious professional should have the following five characteristics:

1. An educated person, the master of some body of knowledge which is neither esoteric nor mundane but essential to ministry and available through accredited educational institutions.
2. An expert person, the master of a specific group of vocational skills.
3. An institutional person, relating to society and serving persons through a social institution, of which the minister is partly a servant and partly a master.
4. A responsible person who "professes" to act competently in any situation that requires the minister's service which includes the highest standard of ethical conduct.
5. A dedicated person who also "professes" to provide something of great value for society.

Joe E. Trull and James Carter conclude this discourse thus:

> *While not demanding that a minister exemplify the notion of the professional in every way, we are convinced that there are good historical and theological reasons for asserting that the Christian minister is a professional. If this is the case, then the recovery of the religious and social meaning of the clergy vocation and profession can revitalize the Church as well as build a foundation for an ethical ministry.*

Having established the professionalism of an ideal gospel minister, we can now go ahead to examine other bases for demanding conformity to professional ethics from him. The bases are briefly discussed below

B. Theistic Basis: Theistic is the adjective from the noun "theism". Harrison (1960:516) describes theism as belief in any god or gods of any kind: Pantheism, henotheism, monolatry, polytheism, and animism. For the purpose of this work, the definition is limited to Christian theism. This is the belief in the God of the Judeo-Christian tradition as revealed in the Bible. The theistic basis for ministerial ethics is based on the nature of God. The Westminster shorter catechism summarily described God thus: "God is a spirit, infinite, eternal, unchangeable in his being, wisdom, power, holiness, justice, goodness and truth".

The theistic basis for ethical demands from church workers is not out of order here because Christian missionary duty should be matched with the nature of God. Missions is theo-centric (God-centred). Highlighting how the Christian missionary enterprise is dependent on the nature of God, Speer (1910:18) maintains:

> *The supreme arguments for missions are not found in any specific words. It is in the very being and character of God that the deepest ground for the missionary enterprise is to be found. We cannot think of God except in terms which necessitates the missionary idea. Though words may reveal the eternal missionary duties, the grounds are in the very being and thoughts of God, in the character of Christianity, in the aim and purpose of the Christian Church, and in the nature of humanity, its unity, and its need.*

Since in this book we are dealing with ethics which has to do with morality, we need to know the moral attributes of God. Pearlman (1973:63) and Wilmington (1984:601-608) enumerate the moral attributes of God as:

1. God is holy
2. God is righteous
3. God is faithful
4. God is merciful
5. God is love

6. God is kind
7. God is true
8. God is light
9. God is good
10. God is gracious
11. God is just
12. God is one

The above moral attributes of God and those not mentioned compel anybody working for him at any level and capacity to follow ethical principles of church work. Each of the above moral attributes of God and its relationship to church work is highlighted below.

God is Holy: Holiness known as "chadosh" in Old Testament Hebrew and "hagios" in New Testament Greek in reference to man simply means separation from what is sinful and consecration unto God. As applied to God, holiness has been defined by Harrison and others (1960:269) thus: "It signifies (a) his separation from, and transcendency over all his creation. It defines his supremacy, majesty, and awesome glory, as in Ex.3:4, 5 and (b) the ethical spotlessness of his character as in Lev.11:44, repeated in 1 Peter 1:16".

In these scriptures, God declared his holy nature and his demand for holiness from his children in these words:

> *Do not defile yourselves by any of these creatures. Do not make yourselves unclean by means of them or be made unclean by them. I am the Lord your God; consecrate yourselves and be holy, because I am holy. Do not make yourselves unclean by any creature that moves on the ground. I am the Lord who brought you out of Egypt to be your God; therefore, be holy because I am holy. As obedient children, do not conform to the evil desires you had when you lived in ignorance. But just as he who called you is holy, so be holy in all you do; for it is written: "Be holy because I am holy (Levetcus 11:43-45; 1 Peter14-16)*

The holiness of God demands that his work at all levels and segments be done in holiness if they are to be acceptable to him and rewarded by him. Church work ethics therefore demands holiness from every church worker and leader.

God is Righteous: God's righteousness has been explained as his holiness in action. It is holiness manifested in his right dealing with his creatures. In defense of his righteousness, God asks in Genesis 18:25, "Shall not the Judge of all the earth do right?"

Righteousness is conformity to the right standard; it is the right conduct in relation to others. In righteousness, God weighs the behaviours and actions of man in relation to himself, his word, and fellow man to ascertain whether they are right or wrong. When man's actions are adjudged by God as being right, that is righteousness; when it is otherwise, it is unrighteousness. Church work ethics demands righteousness from all church workers and leaders.

The church worker should note that the righteous God whose work must be done in righteousness says:

> *Righteousness exalts a nation, but sin is a reproach to any people. The righteous will flourish like a palm tree, they will grow like a cedar of Lebanon planted in the house of the lord, and they will flourish in the courts of our God. They will still bear fruits in old age, they will stay fresh and green proclaiming, "the lord is upright he is my rock, and there is no wickedness in him (Prov.14:34; Psalms 92:12-15)*

God is Just: Justice is a communicable attribute of God manifesting his holiness. Tozer (1997:60) explains God's justice thus:

> *In looking this up very carefully from the Scripture, I find that justice is distinguishable from righteousness in the Old Testament. It's the same root word with variations according to the part of speech used. It*

means uprightness or rectitude. To say that God is just or that the justice of God is a fact is to say that there is uprightness and rectitude in God. Psalm 89:14 says, "Justice and judgment are the habitation of his throne." Justice and righteousness are indistinguishable from each other.

Tozer further posits that justice is not something God has, but something God is. As God is love, God is justice.

Harrison and others classified God's justice as follows:

Relative Justice: This has to do with his rectitude in and of himself.

Absolute Justice: This is the rectitude by which God upholds himself against violations of his holiness.

Rectoral Justice: By rectoral, God institutes righteous laws and establishes just rewards and penalties.

Distributive Justice: By this, God metes out just rewards (remunerative Justice expressing his love) and punishments (retributive justice, justice expressing his wrath).

In regard to man, justice refers to the right rule, conduct, or to each getting his due whether good or bad. Church workers have to be just in their dealings and relationships with their fellow men. The following Bible passages teach and declare the justice of God:

Clouds and thick darkness surround him; righteousness and justice are the foundation of his throne. Then I heard the angel in charge of the waters say, "You are just in these judgments, you who are, who were, the Holy One, because you have so judged; for they have shed the blood of your saints and prophets, and you have given them blood to drink as they deserve. And I heard the altar respond: "Yes, Lord

God Almighty, true and just are your judgments" (Psalms 97:2; Rev.16:5-7)

God is Faithful: God being faithful means that he is absolutely trustworthy with his word being unfailing. Based on his faithfulness, the people of God can have implicit faith in his word and person.

The faithfulness of God is conveyed in the following passages of the Holy Bible:

> *Know therefore that the Lord your God is God; he is the faithful God, keeping his covenant of love to a thousand generations of those who love Him and keep his commandment. Your love, O LORD, reaches to the heavens, your faithfulness to the skies. (Dt 7:9; Ps 36:5).*

Sequel to the fact that faithfulness is the characteristic nature of God, those who work for him should be faithful. No unfaithfulness should be associated with church workers and leaders.

God is Light: God is not only the creator of light; he is the light himself. This statement is conveyed in the following scripture "Every good and perfect gift is from above, coming down from the father of the heavenly lights who does not change like shifting shadows. This is the message we have heard from him and declare to you. God is light in him there is no darkness at all. (James 1:17; 1john 1:5)

In his description of this important missionary nature of God, Peters (1984:58) maintains: *"God is light the Bible declares" (1 John 1:5). This Metaphor is full of meaning, especially as it relates to the outgoing of God and consequently as it relates to missions. The description, "God is light" suggests that God is unapproachable, infinite, unchangeable, perfectly holy, perfectly open, perfectly inviolable, and perfectly true. He is the source of all light, life, goodness, safety, and joy as well as the power of transfiguration for all things. As light, He is also a consuming fire or severe judgment*

Since God is light personally, the workers of God should not live and work in darkness. They are to give natural, supernatural, intellectual, and emotional light to the people both in the church and outside the church. In fact, in doing the work of God, they should have most of the descriptions of divine light mentioned above by Peters.

God is Merciful: God's mercy has been described by Hodges as the divine goodness exercised with respect to the miseries of his creatures, feeling for them, and making provision for their relief, and in the case of impenitent sinners, leading to long-suffering, patience: (Pearlman, 65). In Ps.103:8, the psalmist declared, "The Lord is merciful and gracious, slow in anger and plenteous in mercy".

Mercy is one of the communicable attributes of God which expresses the goodness and love for the guilty and those in miserable condition. The definition of mercy expresses its Old Testament Hebrew word "**hesed**" and its New Testament words "**eloeos**" and "**oiktirmos**" which also mean, pity and compassion. (Harrison; etal:348)

Since God is merciful, church workers and leaders should be merciful. They should not deal with people mercilessly. This viewpoint is supported by Jesus' declaration "Blessed are the merciful; for they shall obtain mercy" (Matthew 5:7)

God Is Love. John the beloved, the apostle of love both in his Gospel and in his Epistle presents God expressly as love. He enjoins believers thus: "Dear friends, let us love one another for love comes from God. Everyone who loves has been born of God and knows God. Whoever does not love, does not know God, because God is love" (1 John 4:7, 8).

> This important nature of God has been succinctly described thus: *Love is the self-imparting quality in the divine nature that leads God to seek the highest good and the most complete possession of his creatures. Love in its highest form is a relation between intelligent,*

moral, and free beings. God's love to man seeks to awaken a responsive love of man to God. In its final form love between God and man, will mean their complete and unrestrained self-giving to each other, and the complete possession of each other by the other (Mullins, 1917:236)

God's love for man has the following characteristics as pointed out by Peters:

- It is outgoing and dynamic
- It is sacrificial and active
- It is comprehensive
- It is a manifold relationship depending on the character, conditions, and needs of its object

The love of God is the agape (sacrificial) kind of love that gives at all costs. It was this agape love that prompted God the Father to give Jesus, his only son as an atoning sacrifice for our sins (John 3:6; John 4:10)

Since God, the owner of the church and church work is love personified. Church workers should do their work in love for God and love one another. Chessman (1997:23) presents the love motives of Christian workers as:

- Love for one's country.
- Love for one's church.
- Love for one's self.
- Love for the people.
- Love for the Lord.

Love for one's country is a very inferior love motive for Christian missionary enterprise. It results in imperialism politically, culturally, religiously, economically, and socially.

Love for one's church is also an inferior love motive for church work. Love for one's self is not ideal love for church workers for Jesus demands self-denial from his followers. Selfishness has destroyed many church workers and leaders.

Love of the people is a good and important motive for church work. It is based on having feelings of compassion for the people being served.

Love of the lord is the highest type of love motive in church work. It shows itself in obedience to God, and desire for Christ's final return.

Having a love for the people and for God is demanded from church workers in church ministerial ethics. In consideration of this view, Griffin (1976:31) posits:

Christian ethical thinkers have usually seen biblical ethics as involving two requirements: love and justice. Love is concerned with the consequences of an action upon the other person. The loving persuader cares about the good or bad that comes from his influence because he cares about the other person as a person. He tries to figure out ahead of time what will happen as a result of his action in order that he might bring about the best possible for the other.

Conclusively, sequel to the loving nature of God, church workers, and leaders should be lovers of God and lovers of the people. Their work and leadership should be characterized by love.

God Is True. The truthful nature of God is conveyed in the scripture which says," Now this is eternal life: that they may know you, the only true God, and Jesus Christ, whom you have sent". Many other passages of the Bible present God as the God of truth. According to A.W, Strong, truth is "that attribute of the divine nature in virtue of which God's being and God's knowledge eternally conform to each other". Truth is anything factual about God. God being true in his moral attribute means that there is no falsehood, deception, or hypocrisy in him. Hence in Numbers 23:19, Balaam the controversial prophet declared:

"God is not a man, that he should lie, nor a son of man that he should change his mind. Does he speak and then not do it? Does he promise and not fulfil?"

The true nature of God demands that church workers and leaders be truthful always. They should speak the truth and avoid falsehood and hypocrisy. Whereas the devil is a liar and the father of lies, Jesus is the truth. His followers and servants must be like him in truthfulness.

God is Good: The psalmist says "Give thanks to the Lord for his is good, his love endures forever". The goodness of God is that his attribute by reason of which he imparts life and other blessings to his creatures (Pearlman, 65).

A.W. Strong explains God's goodness as "The eternal principle of God's nature which leads him to communicate of his own life and blessings to those who are like him in moral character". Due to the fact that God is absolutely morally good, he is not responsible for anything evil. Evil exists by his permission. By God's goodness, he can overrule evil for good.

Church workers and leaders are expected to be like good God by being good to the people they are serving. Shakespeare once said that "an evil soul producing a holy witness is like a goodly apple rotten at the heart". A church worker that is not good but evil, is like a rotten apple that should be thrown away. Ministerial ethics centres on good behaviours and practices in ministry.

God is One: The Hebrew Shema declares
"Hear O Isreal the Lord our God, the Lord is one" (Deut 6:4). The oneness of God means:

(a) Outside God, there is no other God. Any other thing people worship are idols.

(b) God is one in three persons: The Father, The Son, and The Holy Spirit. This is theologically known as the Trinity. The true doctrine of three persons in one God (Trinity) has been explained thus:

> *Convenient designation for one God self-revealed in scriptures as Father, Son, and Holy Spirit. It signifies that within the one essence of the Godhead, we have to distinguish three "persons" who are neither three gods on one side, nor three parts or modes of God on the other, but coequally and coeternally God (Harrison, et al, 531).*

The three persons of the one Godhead: the Father, the Son, and the Holy Spirit are coequal, coeternal and coexistent. They cooperate with each other and do their work in oneness without opposing one another.

Church workers and leaders should be like the One God in compound unity. They should work together in unity without opposing and fighting one another. That is the will of God. Jesus prayed," I have given them the glory that you gave me, that they may be one as we are one" (John 17:22).

C. Missiological Basis: This has to do with the nature of the mission of the Church in the world. The nature of the mission of the Church relevant to our subject matter: ministerial ethics is found in the following scriptural passages:

> *You are the salt of the earth. But if the salt loses its saltiness, how can it be made salty again? It is no longer good for anything, except to be thrown out and trampled by men. You are the light of the world. A city on a hill cannot be hidden. Neither do people light a lamp and put it under a bowl. Instead, they put it on its stand and it gives light to everyone in the house. In the same way, let your light shine before men, that they may see your good deeds and praise your Father in heaven (Mathew 5:13-16).*

The salt and light ministries of the Church to the bitter and dark world inevitably involve a commitment to the ethical principles of the ministry. At Saul's conversion on the road to Damascus, Jesus said to him:

> *Now get up and stand on your feet. I have appeared to you to appoint you as a servant and as a witness of what you have seen of me and what I will show you… I am sending you to them to open their eyes and turn them from darkness to light and from the power of Satan to God, so that they may receive forgiveness of sins and a place among those who are sanctified by faith in me (Acts 26:16-18).*

Church leaders and worker are called by God to open people's eyes and turn them from darkness to light and from sin to righteousness. Such a worker must be morally sound which involves ethical principles. The missionary mandate of the church is more than offering peoples of the world spiritual salvation. The missionary work of the church includes social action which Claerbaut categorized as:

- Social Reconstruction which identifies with the poor and the oppressed to liberate them and change their conditions.
- Social Relief which identifies with the less privileged and through works of mercy render them relief to alleviate their sufferings.
- Social Reform which identifies society's malignancies and reforms unjust social institutions that engender suffering.

Farley was in total support of the fact that the church in its missionary calling has more than spiritual salvation to offer posits:

> It was especially the social gospel of the early twentieth century that pressed the issue of the social character of the gospel. While its frame work was optimism and progressivism which few people now share, its legacy is at work when the church takes its stand against dehumanization movements of modern culture, when it confronts racism, and sexism within itself and the larger society when it debates

issues of militarism and the pollution of the planet. Rare now is the view that the gospel is simply a message about trans-earthly destiny of individual souls. Few doubt that the Christian gospel has something to do with systematic evil and our social well-being.

Therefore, going by the nature of the Church's mission to the world described above from the Bible and the views of different scholars and missiologists there must be conformity to ministerial ethics in carrying out the mission of the church in the world.

d. Ecclesiological Basis: Ecclesiological basis for Church ministerial ethics deals with the ethical nature of the Church. The nature of the Church that elicits conformity to ethical norms includes:

- It is the body of the called-out ones from darkness into light, from sin into righteousness, and from the kingdom of Satan into the kingdom of God ·It is the ground and pillar of truth.
- It is the salt and light of the world.
- It is Christ's ambassador in the world.
- It is the moral watch dog of the society.

The ethical nature of the Church that elicits commitment to ministerial ethics can be concluded in the assertion of Myers (1999:127) thus:

> *First, the role of the Church in transformational development is the same as ours: to be a servant and source of encouragement, not a commander or a judge. Second, the Church can and must be a source of value formation within the community. When the Church is its best, it is a sign of the values of the kingdom and is contributing holistic discipline to the community for its well-being. Finally, the Church is the hermeneutical community that reads the biblical story as its story and applies this story to the concrete circumstances of its time, place and culture.*

It is not only the ethical nature of the church that elicits conformity to ministerial ethics by church workers and leaders. Responsibilities of the church also elicit that. These responsibilities as enumerated by Wilmington include:

- It is to love God.
- It is to Glorify God.
- It is to display God's grace.
- It is to evangelize the world.
- It is to baptize believers.
- It is to instruct believers.
- It is to edify believers.
- It is to discipline believers.
- It is to provide fellowship for believers.
- It is to care for its own in time of need.
- It is to provoke Israel to jealousy.
- It is to provide rulers for the millennial kingdom.
- It is to act as a restraining and enlightening force in this present world.
- It is to promote all that is good.

The above responsibilities of the church make it imperative for its workers and leaders to be committed to Christian work ethics. Without such commitment, the Church will fail in its responsibilities to God and to the society.

e. **Anthropological Basis:** This has to do with the origin of man and his moral nature. Those who believe in the special creative theory of man's origin as against the evolutionary theory accept the fact that man has a moral nature. Pearlman (1937:41) posits that man's life is regulated by conceptions of right and wrong which enables him to know the right course of action to follow and the wrong course to avoid. God, who created man in his image, is a moral law giver who gave man conscience to know right and wrong. He designed a standard of conduct for man and made man's nature capable of understanding that code of conduct. In the light of the afore-said, any man working for God is expected of God and man to conform to ethical standards. Emmanuel Kant, the German philosopher once said, "Two things fill my soul with awe: the starry heavens above me and the moral law within me" (Pearlman, 42). The moral law within the Church worker coupled with the Spirit and word of God in him compels him to conform to all ethical standards of the Church and its ministry.

f. **Biblical Basis:** This point examines whether the demand for ethical behaviour from Church leaders and workers is Bible-based. Biblical basis for ethical conformity should be examined because both conservative Protestantism and the Roman Catholic Church recognize the Bible as the voice of God to humanity. While Conservative Protestantism recognises the Bible as solar fidei regular (that is, the only authoritative voice of God to man). The Roman Catholic and the Eastern Oriental Churches regard it as the prima fidei regular (that is, the primary voice of God to man) (Ram, 1970:1).

The old and new testaments are full of passages that call for good moral behaviours from the people. In fact, the entire Bible is a book on ethics. The historical, prophetic, poetic books, the gospel and the epistles contain ethical injunctions for man. The Ten Commandments in the book of Exodus, is a compendium of ethical injunctions of Judaism and Christianity. The prophets and the apostles were vanguards of religious ethics. In Philippians 4:8, we find this Paul's conclusive ethical injunction:

> *Finally, brothers, whatever is true, whatever is noble, whatever is right, whatever is pure, whatever is lovely, whatever is admirable, if anything is excellent or praiseworthy think about such things.*

Emory A. Griffin (1976:31) sees biblical ethics as involving two requirements: love and justice. Love is concerned with the consequences of an action or inaction upon the other person. Justice deals with universal obligations- the ought and the ought not of life. Since according to biblical ethical thinkers, ethics is all about love and justice which are major themes of the Bible. From all these, it becomes glaring that demands for conformity with ethics in Christian service has biblical backing.

CHAPTER 3

ETHICAL THEORIES AND THE CHURCH MINISTRY

In this chapter we are going to examine concepts of right and wrong which are the subject matters of ethics. Here we ask the question, what is right or wrong? How do we know what is right or wrong? Different Philosophers and Scholars have conceived of right or wrong in different ways. These different conceptions are discussed below:

A. Emotivism:
This theory is based on the saying of the Greek Philosopher, Pythagoras that "Man is the measure of all things". This theory maintains that an action is right or wrong depending on a person's feeling. According to Isiramhen (1998:166), the position of this argument is that an action like abortion is good for those who feel it is good and bad for those who feel it is bad. Going by this theory, the right is what is right to me. What is right to me may be bad for another person.

This theory of morality if accepted will lead to societal chaos; for everyone will do what he feels is right and will avoid only those things he feels are bad. There will be no collective judgement and uniformity of action in the society and in the church.

The minister of the gospel and indeed all Church leaders and workers should not base their actions on their feelings alone. All feelings must be examined in the light of the word of God, the Constitution, and the Bye-Laws of the Church and the laws of the land. Therefore, the theory of emotivism is not in conformity with biblical Christian ethics. In Christian ministry, we do not work by our feeling.

B. Cultural Relativism: Morals are mores Since this theory is based on culture, it is necessary to define culture here. Luzbetak (1963:60) explains culture thus:

> *Culture is a design for living. I t is a plan according to which society adapts itself to its physical, social, and ideational environment. A plan for coping with the physical environment would include such matters as food production and all technological knowledge and skill. Political systems, kinship and family organisation, and law are examples of social adaptation, a plan according to which one is to interact with his fellow man. Man copes with his ideational environment through knowledge, art, magic, science, philosophy, and religion. Cultures are but different answers to essentially the same human problems.*

From the above explanation of Luzbetak, culture has been categorized into technological, sociological and ideological culture (Hesselgrave,1991:101).

Culture is the total way of life of a people. It varies from people to people. Culture is never static. Culture is dynamic as it changes either by growth or by extermination with time. Culture and its traits are relative. The ethical theory of cultural relativism judges right and wrong conducts from the practices of a particular culture. In other words, as what is wrong in one culture may be right in another culture and vice versa, there is no absolute universal right or wrong. Geisler and Feinberg (1980:354) explained morals and mores thus: *Some hold that right is determined by the group to which one belongs. Ethics is identified with the ethnic; moral commands are considered community demands. This of course implies cultural relativity of morality. Any overlapping of ethical principles between cultures and societies that would seem to give the appearance of universality is accidental.*

It is necessary at this juncture to briefly examine culture and biblical absolutes. Culture is the way of life of a people which includes their language, behaviour, thinking pattern, norms and values, food, housing etc. Clock Holm (1949:23) defines culture as "a way of thinking, feeling, believing. It is a groups' knowledge stored up for future use".

A cross-cultural Christian missionary confronts three cultures: his own culture, the respondent culture and the Bible culture. The Bible judges all cultures. No matter how culturally relative morality may be, there are biblical absolutes which cannot be sacrificed on the altar of cultural relativism. In other words, when a particular culture judges a particular behaviour right while the Bible judges it wrong, the judgement of the Bible supersedes. Therefore, cultural relativism as an ethical theory should be weighed in the light of biblical absolutes.

Cultural Relativism has the following problems: making what is the practice in a place what ought to be and the inability to resolve conflicts between peoples of the world as each people will claim being right accordingly their culture.

C. **Voluntarism: What is Legal is Right** This ethical theory maintains that what is right is determined by what the law says. According Isiramen (1998:168), this is a type of ethics which sees the ethical interrelation of facts as having basis on the will of some law maker who determines the rightness or wrongness of values and ways of acting. In voluntaristic ethics, what is right is what is in agreement with codes, for instance, government laws and decrees or religious laws like the ten commandment or Sharia law, and constitution and byelaws of nations or organizations. Furthermore voluntaristic ethics maintains that something is right if it is in line with God's will and vice versa.

The Christian worker should be law abiding. But not all laws are in conformity with God's law and will. The will of God takes precedence over all laws. For instance, in the case of the woman caught in adultery in the Gospel of John chapter 8, the law of Moses prescribes death. In this case, Jesus did not see following the law to be the right thing to do in determining the fate of the woman. On this case the Scripture maintains: *When they kept on questioning him, he straightened up and said to them If any of any of you is without sin, let him be the first to throw stone at her. Again, he stooped down and wrote on the ground. Those who heard it began to go away one at a time, the older ones first, until only Jesus was left with the woman still standing there. Jesus straightened up and asked her, woman, where are they? Has no one condemned you? "No one sir, she said."Then neither do I condemn you, Jesus declared, "Go now and leave your life of sin (John 8:7-11).*

Jesus' action demonstrated that in divine economy, what is legal may not be the right thing to do in certain cases. This is because laws are made for man and not man for laws. Going by the law, the woman was to die but going by grace and mercy, she was forgiven and given opportunity for repentance.

D. **Utilitarianism: The Greatest Good for the Race is Right.**

The major proponent of this ethical theory is John Stuart Mill. This theory maintains that the rightness or the wrongness of an action is determined by the result. Hence, to the

Utilitarian, if the consequences of an action are good, then the action is right or good, but if the consequences are bad, then the action is wrong or bad. To the Utilitarian, where the result of an action is partly good and partly bad, the act that will on the whole give the best result is morally good (Isiramhen, 170). The best result of an action must be understood in quantitative and in qualitative senses.

The gospel minister should understand that good result does not justify all actions. If you do wrong thing to do good to people God will never leave you unpunished.

E. **Machiavellism: Might is Right**

An Italian political thinker of the 15th century, Machiavelli Nicolas is the proponent of this theory. According to him, the right thing a leader should do is to employ force to get what he wants. He should use force to get political power and maintain the position by force. Hence whatever is achieved by might is right. Similar to Machiavelli's view is that of ancient Greek philosopher, Thrasymachus who held that ***"justice is in the interest of the stronger party" (Geisler and Feinberg, 1987:353).***

Summarily, this theory maintains that whatever you achieve by use of power or force is right. This theory does not command popular acceptance because power corrupts and absolute power corrupts absolutely. In the Christian worldview, the right action is not whatever the powerful does. Power and goodness are different. Scriptures abound where the use of power was adjudged as being wrong. For instance, Jacob passing out his will of blessings to his sons said to Simeon and Levi who exhibited their martial manly power and anger on the men of Shechem where their sister, Diana was defiled said to them:

> *Simeon and Levi are brothers-their swords are weapons of violence. Let me not enter their council, let me not join their assembly, for they have killed men in their anger and hamstrung oxen as they pleased. Cursed be their anger, so fierce, and their fury so cruel. I will scatter them in Jacob and disperse them in Israel (Gen.49:5-7)*

F. **Antinomianism: Nothing is Right or Wrong**

This is the ethical theory of some philosophers who are against law in tho society or organizations. It maintains that actions are right or wrong depending on one's feeling. The antinomians also called the nihilist believe that no law should govern any society or organization. People therefore act according to their whims and caprices. The apostle Paul talking about the goodness of law as against the view of the antinomians said:

> *We know that the law is good if one uses it properly. We also know that law is made not for the righteous but for law breakers and rebels, the ungodly and sinful, the unholy and irreligious; for those who kill*

their fathers or mothers, for murderers, for adulterers and perverts, for slave traders and liars and perjurers-and for whatever else is contrary to the sound doctrine that conforms to the glorious gospel of the blessed God, which he entrusted to me (1 Timothy 1:8-10)

The Christian worker believes in law and is law abiding. The God he works for is the universal law giver. Laws that regulate human conducts and operations should not be repudiated by church leaders and workers. The church worker's operations should be in accordance with laws of God, the church and the society.

G. **Hedonism: Right is What Brings Pleasure**

Pearlman explains hedonism thus: Hedonism, from the Greek word meaning "pleasure is a theory of life which maintains that the highest good in life is the securing of pleasure and the avoiding of pain, so that the first question to be asked is not, "Is it right?" but "Will it bring pleasure?"

Hedonism is also called Epicureanism which is a system of philosophy based chiefly on the teachings of the Greek philosopher, Epicurus. The essential doctrine of Epicureanism is that pleasure is the supreme good and main goal of life. Intellectual pleasures are preferred to sensual ones, which tend to disturb peace of mind. True happiness according to Epicurus is the serenity resulting from the conquest of fear of the gods, of death, and of the afterlife. The ultimate aim of all epicurean speculation about nature is to rid people of such fears (Microsoft Encarta).

The simplest explanation of this ethical theory which is credited to the epicureans of the 4th century BC is that any action that brings pleasure is right and what brings pain is wrong. The Christian worker should not be guided by this epicurean or hedonistic theory. The Bible condemns loving pleasure instead of loving God. This is because not all pleasures are good and not all pains are bad. Pleasures of sin are bad and pains of hard work are good.

H. **Moderation is Right:**

According to the Greek philosopher, Aristotle, the meaning of right is found in moderation which is called "the golden mean". For the propounder of this theory, moderate course between two extreme actions is the right course of action. The problem here is that sometimes the right action calls for extreme action. Not all moderation is right in the light of the word of God. Moderation of bad is still bad and evil.

I. **Situationism: Situation Determines the Right.**

This theory maintains that an action is judged right or wrong depending on the situation the actor finds himself and his good will. In the words of Isiramen, the location of moral goodness according to the situationist is in the upright attitude of the person that is acting. Situational ethics justifies many actions that are condemnable going by faith and the law.

We can summarize this section in the word of Feinberg (359):

> One solution to the problem of defining good or right is to proclaim that something is right if God wills it right and wrong if He wills it wrong. This would solve the problem of determining content in the meaning of good, as well as the difficulty involved in defining good in terms of something not ultimate. Christians claim God's sovereign will is ultimate and the Bible spells out the content of that will to us.

In the light of Feinberg's view and Christian ethics, whatever is adjudged right must agree with God's will which is spelt out in the Bible. Every ethical theory must be weighed on the scale of biblical ethics.

CHAPTER 4

ETHICAL CONDUCTS IN CHRISTIAN MINISTRY

The Oxford Advanced Learner's Dictionary: International Students' Edition defines the adjective "ethical" as "Morally correct or acceptable". This chapter deals with conducts that are morally correct, acceptable and are therefore expected of all those in Christian service whether on full time or part time basis. These ethical conducts are also expected from all church workers and leaders at all levels and ministries. The following are the code of conduct expected of all church leaders and workers.

4.1 Hard Work:

It is necessary to point out from the onset that our God is a hard worker. He believes in hard work and encourages it. In six days he created the universe and everything in it and rested on the seventh day when the work of creation was finished (Onyeije, 1992:107). Stressing on the importance of hard-work in leadership Newman (1997:51,52) posits:

> True success comes from hard work. There are no short cuts. Leadership success is having a dream then work, work, work. Learn to love work. There are so many in hospitals that would do anything to get out with a healthy body and work. Work is a principle that God has given to man. Even before Adam sinned against God, God placed him in the Garden of Eden to keep it. Success is hard work in disguise. Success, work, and discipline all go together.

Every Church leader and worker is expected by God and men to be committed to hard work in the following areas:

Spiritual Hard Work: Spiritual hard work deals with consulting God through prayers to know what to do and how to do the work of God. The work of the ministry is not done by presumption or according to the will of man. God must be consulted to know his will. In the passage below, God rebuked the Israelites who carried out their plans according to their will without consulting God to know his will:

> Woe to the obstinate children, declares the LORD, to those who carry out plans that are not mine, forming an alliance, but not by my spirit, heaping sin upon sin; who go down to Egypt without consulting me; who look for help to Pharaoh's protection; to Egypt's shade for refuge. But Pharaoh's protection will be to your shame, Egypt's shade will bring you disgrace (Isaiah 30:1-3)

Due to the fact that it is "heaping sin upon sin" for one to enter into any alliance-including ministerial alliance without consulting God, every church worker must pray through and ascertain God's will in whatever one is doing in the church. It is unethical not to do so. On the day Jesus met Paul of Tarsus on his way to Damascus to persecute the members of the early church, he asked the all-important question: "What shall I do Lord?" Church leaders and workers should learn from Paul and always find out from God what he wants us to do in every work and situation.

Mental Hard Work: This dimension of hard work has to do with thinking and reasoning on how to succeed in the work of God we are doing. Becoming a Christian and the presence of the Holy Spirit in the believer do not mean kissing good bye to one's brain and thinking. In Isaiah 1:18 the Lord says, "Come now, let us reason together" This reasoning together involves thinking. Discussing on how to succeed in any life's endeavour, Peale (1986:115) posits, "think and think and think some more and, to thinking, add prayer; these two procedures are miracle workers".

The importance of mental hard work through thinking process is demonstrated in the rational- field- selection method for world evangelization. Fraser and Dayton (1990:63) explain rational field selection thus:

> Rational field selection is a choice governed principally by a consciously rational process. This involves gathering information and experience and weighing alternatives in the light of given goals. An intellectually demonstrated need and opportunity matrix determine the choice.

From the aforesaid, it is very clear that mental hard work is very ethical in church work and vice versa. The Scripture in Proverbs 19:15 rightly said that an idle mind will suffer hunger.

Physical Hard Work: God, the owner of the church and the work exhorts his children to work hard physically in these words, "Whatever your hand finds to do, do it with all your might, for in the grave, where you are going, there is neither working nor planning nor knowledge nor wisdom" (Ecclesiastes 9:10). Following mental hard work is the physical hard work. The physical dimension of hard work is executory in nature. It has to do with using the whole of one's energy to do a particular work within the least possible time.

Below is divine exhortation to hard work to church workers in particular and to all humans in general:

> *Go to the ant, you sluggard: consider its ways and be wise.... How long will you lie there, you sluggard? When will you get up from your sleep? A little sleep, a little slumber a little folding of the hands to rest and poverty will come on you like a bandit and scarcity like an armed man (Prov. 6:6-11).*

Both in the Old and New Testaments, God enjoins his people to work hard. Church workers and leaders entrusted with God's work should be dedicated and committed to hard work. After all, all hard works bring profit (Prov. 14:23). An excerpt of the Unitarian ministerial code of ethics is relevant here:

> The minister should always place service above profits, avoiding the suspicion of an inordinate love of money and never measuring his work by his salary. He should be conscientious in giving full time and strength to the work of his church, engaging in vocations and other occupation in such away and to such a degree as not to infringe unduly upon the work unless some definite arrangement for part-time service is made with the church.

From the above excerpt salient ethical conducts stand out clearly:

- The church minister should be committed to service demonstrated in hard work.
- He should not base his service on his salary which might be meagre.
- He should give full strength and time to his work unless he is a part timer.
- He should not be involved in another work that will affect his church work negatively unless he was employed on part time basis.
- If he has extra church work, his leaders should know about it.

The above points should apply to all ministers of the gospel irrespective of their denominations. This will be for the good of the church. It will also be of help and blessing to the minister.

4.2 Diligence (Excellence):

Diligence or excellence means doing something that is very good and of high quality. God, our maker is diligent and excellent in all his ways and dealings with man. In diligence and excellence, he did his creative work and certified it as being good (Genesis 1:21). Since God is diligent and excellent in his work and dealings with man, his workers, church workers and leaders are expected to be diligent in their work. Carelessness and shoddiness in the work of God is unethical. In proverbs 22:29 the Scripture maintains “Seest thou a man diligent in his business?” he shall stand before kings; he shall not stand before mean men”. If diligence is required in our business, more diligence is required in God's business as we shall stand before God, the owner of the work to give account.

An excellence and diligent church worker will serve among kings and noble men through promotion. Daniel's origin was not, an obstacle to his promotion in Babylon because excellence was found in his spirit and work. (Daniel 6:3-5).
As an excellent worker, Daniel had the following qualities:

- He distinguished himself by exceptional qualities
- No corruption was found in him
- He was trust worthy
- He was not negligent
- Faults and errors were not found in him.
- He was faithful.

Church leaders should recognize excellent workers, encourage and use them, instead of avoiding them.

4.3. Regularity and Punctuality by Prudent Time Management
Truancy, absenteeism, and lateness to duty, work, and meetings are unethical behaviours in church business. This calls for prudent time management. Dealing with leaders and time management, Newman maintains that time is your most valuable personal resource. Use it wisely because it can't be replaced. Time management skills can be developed and perfected. It will lead to greater productivity and performance. When you control your time, you accomplish important goals and free up your nights and weekends for other family activities. Controlling your time helps overcome frustration and brings your life into balance giving you the feeling of control and poise. Better planning of your time enables you to give yourself more to others. You will feel better on top of the pile than under it. Life will take on a greater zest, enthusiasm and productivity. You will be able to handle a crisis far more easily, and it will give you more time for planning (106, 110).

The scriptures— Ecclesiastes 3:1 and Ephesians 5:16 deal with prudent time management. God the creator of time says in the above passages that he has set time for everything under heaven and time should not be misused by man. Church leaders and indeed all Christians are managers of God's time which they must account for.

The Western linear concept of time should be adopted by church leaders and workers instead of the African cyclical concept. In the Western concept of time, time is regarded as a straight line which when lost, cannot be recovered and must therefore not be wasted. In the African concept, time is regarded to be cyclical in nature which when lost can be recovered again.

African cyclical concept of time makes for lateness, absenteeism and time wastage which are all unethical in leadership and church business. Benjamin Franklin (1706-1790) one of the founding fathers of America once said, "Do you love life? Then do not squander time for that is the stuff life is made of". In the words of Lakein (2003:1): "Time is life. It is irreversible and irreplaceable. To waste regular time is to waste your life, but to master your time is to master life and make most use of it".

As masters of their time and their lives, church leaders and workers are expected as a matter of ministerial ethics to be punctual and regular to duties and meetings. They must shun absenteeism, lateness, truancy and time wastage.

4.4 Integrity:

This means being honest, sincere, truthful, and maintaining a good name. God is interested in the integrity of Christian workers and leaders as seen in 1 Kings 9:4-5 where God charged Solomon saying:

> *As for you, if you walk before me in the integrity of heart and uprightness as David your father did, and do all I command and observe all my decrees and laws, I will establish your royal throne over Israel forever as I promised David your father.*

Swindol quoted by Noyce (1988:23-24) explains integrity thus:

> When one has integrity there is an absence of hypocrisy. He or she is personally reliable, financially accountable, and privately clean and innocent of impure motives. Integrity includes both who one is and what one does. It is ethical soundness, intellectual veracity and moral excellence. It keeps us from fearing the white light of close examination and from resisting the scrutiny of accountability. It is honesty at all cost, and a rocklike character that won't crack when standing alone, or crumble when pressure mounts.

In the above scripture, in as much as God recognized and appreciated the great temple Solomon built for him, he demanded integrity from him. God made integrity conditionality for the establishment and continuation of his royal throne. No matter the height of leadership position one is occupying no matter the great work a person does for God in the church integrity is a necessity for divine approval and blessing. Harping on the need for Christian workers to have the virtue of integrity, Murphy (2000:63) maintains that integrity in a Christian is a priceless treasure and that is doubly so for Christian leaders and that there is no truly great and powerful Christian leader who does not walk in godly integrity. God always ultimately greatly blesses his leaders of integrity. The importance of integrity in church work and leadership is highlighted by Eisenhower thus:

> In order to be a leader a man must have followers. And to have followers, a man must have their confidence. Hence, the supreme quality for the leader is unquestionably integrity. Without it, no real success is possible. No matter whether it is on a section gang, a football field, in the army, or in an office, if a man's associates find him guilty of being phoney, if they find he lacks forthright integrity, he will fail. His teachings and actions must square with each other. The first great need, therefore, is integrity and high purpose.

If you want to be a person of integrity watch out and be mindful of the four FS (4fs): fame, female, finance, and food. Remember that food gained by fraud tastes sweet to a man but he ends up with a mouth full of gravel (Prov.
20:17). The following guideline given by Newman for maintaining integrity can be of help to the church worker and leader:

1. Be a person who honours your word.
2. Do not lie to cover facts. Nothing increases compatibility like mutual trust and honesty Credibility is hard to regain.
3. Watch the bribes that may compromise your position.
4. Be responsible for your mistakes and learn from them. "Do not pass heat on others" for your mistakes.
5. Guard your tongue. Do not divulge information given in confidence.

4.5 Loyalty

Loyalty means, being true, faithful, obedient and submissive to a constituted authority or an institution. The following are the areas of the church worker's loyalty.

Loyalty to God: The church worker is a person called by God. The church worker is called by God either on a full-time or part-time basis. Church workers and leaders are under an obligation to be loyal to God. They should be faithful and submissive to God totally. In his loyalty to God, the preacher must faithfully be God's oracle. Balaam in his loyalty said "If Balak gives me his palace filled with silver and gold… I must say only what the Lord says" (Numbers 24:13). He who pays the piper dictates the tune, says an adage. The church worker is rewarded and maintained by God. In eternity, he will be rewarded by God. He must therefore be loyal to God.

Loyalty to a constituted Authority: A constituted authority exists in the form of elected or appointed leaders of the church at all levels. Our loyalty to God is demonstrated by our obedience, submission and faithfulness to our leaders. God commands us to be loyal to our leaders. It is unethical to be confrontational and rebellious against our leaders. The following scripture lays credence to this:

> *Everyone must submit himself to the governing authorities for there is no authority except that which God has established. The authorities that exist have been established by God. Consequently, he who rebels against the authority is rebelling against what God has instituted, and those who do so will bring judgment on themselves (Romans 13:1-2).*

Leadership and Church work ethics require loyalty to the church authority under which the worker works. Disloyalty disqualifies a church worker or leader.

Loyalty to the church: When we speak of loyalty to the church, we mean the love, faithful obedience and submission church workers owe their denominations, local churches and their departments. The worker's loyalty to his church is manifested in:

i. Faithfulness to the church's doctrine, in word, teaching and conduct.
ii. Faithfulness in attending and promoting church regular and occasional programmes.
iii. Faithfulness in financial support of the church through giving and tithing in recognition of the fact that God is the sole owner of money. (Hagai 2:8)
iv. Faithfulness in rendering services in the church
v. Accepting transfers and redeployment.
vi. Presenting the good, not the bad image of your church to the public.
viii. Following the officially laid down procedure in the ministers' handbook in officiating wedding ceremonies especially the marital oath.

Loyalty to System of Church Government: It is well understood that the Church is not only an organism, it is also an organisation. As an organisation, it requires government. God instituted human government having known its importance in the smooth running and operation of human society. Discussing the dispensation and institution of human government, Ndukwe (1998;37) posits:

> It started under Noah after the flood and ended, and with the confusion of language at the tower of Babel. After the flood, man was commanded to "replenish the earth". He chose to settle at a place. God confused man's language and caused him to scatter upon the earth, it lasted about 400 years.

As God was very interested in having a human government, he is equally interested in having a church government. Church leaders and scholars have identified four kinds of church government:

- Episcopalian
- Presbyterianism
- Congregationalism
- Presbyterianism/Congregationalism.

Each of these types of church government shall be briefly discussed for the benefit of church leaders and workers involved in church administration.

Episcopalism: This is the system of church government by the bishops who exercise sole and ultimate authority. The authority of the bishop is pressed through his subordinates or lower hierarchies down to the congregation. The authority of the bishop is not questioned. The churches that operate this system of government include Roman Catholic, Anglican and other neo-Pentecostal denominations with general overseers as their heads.

Presbyterianism: This is the system of church government in which a body of elders governs the church. This system of church government has been further explained thus:

> The government of the church is given to a body of elders either elected or appointed by the church. These elders have equal powers, although the government is headed by a chairman whose position is

that of the first among equals. Decisions are reached by a consensus opinion of members.

The Presbyterian church is well known for the Presbyterian system of church government.

Congregationalism: In this system of church government, the congregation not the clergy govern the church. The congregation chooses its leaders and pastoral leaders. The running of the church is very much dependent on the decision of the congregation. The Baptist Church is known for this type of church government.

Presbyterianism/Congregationalism: This system of church governing is simply a combination of Presbyterianism and congregationalism. As the name implies, the church is governed by the body of elders in conjunction with the congregation. The congregation is usually represented by a group of men which may be called deacons. The pastors and deacons join together to elect leaders at certain level of the church and at the local church level. The pastors and all the bonafide members of the congregation elect their leaders. Assemblies of God church is well known for its Presbyterian/congregational system of church government.
A question is pertinent here: which system of church government is the best and acceptable to God? All the church government system has biblical backing. Every denomination should operate a system that will make for the smooth running and growth of the church. Whichever church government is adopted, it must have the following biblical principles according to Gangel (1981:26):

- It must be spiritual in function.
- It should be representative in function.
- It should be biblical in constitution.
- It should be participatory in form.

Gangel emphasizing on the fact that any church government must be participatory in form maintains:

> The existence of numerous evangelical denominations with varying attitudes regarding church government is a demonstration that the scriptures are not explicit on the issue. Some interpret the New Testament to teach congregational government, others favour the Presbyterian form, and still others the hierarchical Episcopalian structure. Quite obviously, each group will defend its preference from scripture and history. The only point I wish to make here, therefore is the renewed emphasis on the church as people. Evidence throughout the book of Acts strongly suggests that whatever emphasis may have been placed on the role of elders, the New Testament church leaders never forgot the participatory role of people in the operation of the church. That was an omission brought about by the later corruption of medieval forms.

One of the causes of conflict in church leadership is disloyalty to the system of church government enshrined in the constitution and in the bylaws of the church. To avoid conflict and crisis in the church, the church leader and worker is hereby advised to be loyal and maintain the type of church government the church is known for. If there is a need for change in the system of church government, the change should be done but by the entire membership of the church through their representatives in general council meetings (Synod) of the church.

4.6 Commitment to Servant Leadership Before examining the implication of servant leadership, let us answer the question: What is leadership? According to John Adair, leadership is working as a senior partner with other members to achieve the task, build the team and meet individual needs.

According to Ukeje (1992; 195), The function of organizational leadership is to influence the group toward the achievement of group goals by planning, organizing, directing, and integrating the institutional demands and needs of members in a way that will be both productive and individually fulfilling.

John Maxwell (2008:11) makes the following descriptions about leadership:

- Leadership is the willingness to put one's self at risk.
- Leadership is being dissatisfied with the current reality.
- Leadership is seeing the possibilities in a situation while others are seeing the limitations.
- Leadership is the readiness to stand out in a crowd.
- Leadership is the integration of the heart, head and soul.
- Leadership is inspiring others with a vision of what they can contribute.

Servant leadership is both the Old and New Testaments pattern of leadership approved by God who appoints leaders.

Osei-Mensah (1990:9) highlighting biblical models for leadership maintains:

> We find this model applied to all legitimate leadership in the Bible. In both the Old and New Testaments those who are qualified for appointment as leaders among the people of God are always appointed to serve whether appointed as prophets, priests or kings. They are not to lord it over God's people but to serve them.

The facts enumerated below elucidate the point that the biblical model for leadership is servant leadership:

> *God was very much pleased with Solomon at the beginning of his reign because he manifested the spirit of servant leadership when he requested for wisdom for serving the people with justice. Solomon saw his kingly position not as an opportunity to serve himself but to serve God's people and please God (1 Kings 3:9-10).*

The garment worn by Aaron the high priest, depicted service to God's people. On the priestly garment of Aaron was engraved twelve precious stones containing the name of the twelve tribes of Israel. Which covered his two shoulders. Also, arranged in the breastplate put over his priestly robes were individual precious stones bearing the names of the twelve tribes of Israel. Therefore, in the vestment of the high priest of Israel, he carried the names of the twelve tribes of Israel on his two shoulders and on his heart when he came before the Lord. These were symbols of continual intercession for them (Exodus 28: 29). The role of the high priest was that of a servant leader attending to the spiritual needs of God's people.
The Old Testament prophets of the Lord were called servants. This was because they served for the benefit of the people of God. The prophets brought God's messages to the people.

In the New Testament, Jesus set forth the biblical model of servant leadership in word and indeed. In Mathew 20:25-28 he presented himself as a servant leader who wanted his followers to be servant leaders when he said, "You know that the rulers of the Gentiles lord it over them, and their high officials exercise authority over them. It should not be so with you. Instead, whoever wants to become great among you must be your servant; and whoever wants to be first must be your slave, just as the son of man did not come to be served but to serve and to give his life as a ransom for many."

Osei-Mensah rightly observed that throughout Jesus' ministry, especially in his relationship with his disciples, he consistently modelled servant leadership which should be followed by his followers. Janvier and Thaba (1997) explain servant leadership thus:

> Servant leadership aspires for biblical objectives and purposes in a Christian organization. It also reflects biblical processes and ways of dealing with people. Its motives reflect biblical qualities. It is such a servant leader who is never full of his own schemes, plans and ways of doing his things. Instead like Jesus Christ, God's starting point is

his starting point. A servant leader uses his power or influence to glorify God, edify, comfort, encourage, heal, bless and bring about justice.

Commitment to servant leadership is a necessity for the smooth running of the Church and ministries of the church. All church leaders and workers should see themselves as servants and commit themselves to serving. This is what our master, Jesus taught and modelled.

Servant leaders have the following characteristics:

Humble Service:
This is one of the hallmarks of servant leadership. Jesus demonstrated this when he stooped down in humility and washed the feet of his disciples. The Bible recorded this episode thus:

> *Jesus knew that the Father had put all things under his power, and that he had come from God and was returning to God; so, he got up from the meal, took off his outer clothing, and wrapped a towel around his waist. After that, he poured water into a basin and began to wash his disciples' feet drying them with the towel that was wrapped around him. (John 13:3,4).*

Servant leaders must be like Jesus in humbling themselves and rendering service.

Group Membership: A servant leader does not see himself as distinct and separate from the people he leads. Jesus our model-servant leader never separated himself from his disciples and followers, even in dressing. A servant leader sees himself as a member of the group he leads, not as their lord above and separate from them.

Consultation: Servant leaders do not work alone. They operate participatory administration by consulting co-leaders to seek their opinions on certain issues that concern the organization. A wise servant leader knows decisions and actions he cannot take without consulting those leading the organization with him.

Delegation of Duty: Due to his humble and selfless nature, a servant leader sees something good in others and therefore gives them the opportunity to use and develop their gifts. He does this through delegation of duties. In the words of Osei-Mensah, "The first example of deficient leadership is the overly conscientious leader, who hugs leadership responsibilities to himself, sure that no one else could carry them as a result he wears out both himself and those he leads".
Sequel to the fact that every member of the church is gifted and nobody is indispensable, servant leaders should delegate responsibilities. By this, gifts are used and developed.

Teachableness: One of the characteristics of servants is openness and willingness to learn. A servant leader is willing to be taught what he does not know by those he leads. Being a leader does not mean knowing everything. A servant leader has a teachable spirit and does not feel threatened when new ideas are being presented by someone else.

Accessibility and Approachability:
Accessibility is the leader's ability to make himself available to his own people. Approachability is the ability of the leader to receive and welcome people who come to him by virtue of his leadership position. A leader who wishes to be successful with the people he leads must make an effort to be accessible and approachable. These are among the characteristics of servant leaders. Jesus was accessible and approachable even to children.

Exemplary and Sacrificial Service:
In the words of Osei-Mensah,

The third prerequisite for leadership in addition to conservation and to a renewal of mind, is a life of exemplary obedience. We must first be an example in relation to the Lordship of Christ. The authority a leader exercises in the church is derived. Jesus Christ is the sovereign head and ultimate authority in his church. He is not an absentee Lord. He said to his disciples, "I will be with you always, to the very end of the age" (Mathew 28:20).

The people we are called upon to lead are more likely to co-operate and submit, if they know it is to the Lord they are submitting and if they see us showing the way by bowing our own knees to King Jesus. We have no right to call for the submission of others if we ourselves are not submitted to the king.

John C. Maxwell rightly observed that a leader knows the way goes the way and shows the way. This implies that a leader must be an example to those being led. This is very much one of the characteristics of servant leadership. A servant leader does not act as a big boss and hand down a set of rules, commands, and duties he is not involved in carrying out. Rather, he shows an example in keeping rules and in performing duties.

Describing the attitude of a good shepherd Jesus said "When he has brought out all his own, he goes on ahead of them, and his sheep follow him because they know his voice" (John 10:4)

Going ahead of the people that are led, and practicing exemplary living is an invaluable attitude of a servant leader. In the words of Jesus, "The good shepherd lays down his life for the sheep". This is all about making sacrifices. The servant leader does not only render an exemplary service. He renders sacrificial service. He sacrifices time, energy, money, sleep, pleasure, comfort, etc., all for the good of the people and the organization.

Selflessness: A servant leader is selfless. He places the interest of the people and organization he is leading above his personal interest. He has been crucified with Christ and has died to self, so he is no more a victim of self-assertion, self-projection and inordinate ambition for fame, ecclesiastical position, power and money. The Apostle Paul was reflecting on this when he said, "I have been crucified with Christ and I no longer live but Christ lives in me. The life I live in the body, I live by faith in the son of God who loved me and gave himself for me" (Galatians 2:20).

Without selflessness, servant leadership is a utopia or a mirage. All those wishing to be servant leaders must yield themselves to be crucified with Christ.
Other attributes that characterize servant leaders include:

- Accountability
- Prudent use of resources
- Record Keeping
- Ability to listen to others - Acceptance of criticism

4.7. Discipline:

In his book, *Spiritual Leadership,* Oswald J. Sanders writing on discipline as a qualification for leadership said:

> Only the disciplined person will rise to his highest powers. He is able to lead because he has conquered himself. The words disciple and discipline are derived from the same root. A leader is a person who has first submitted willingly and learned to obey a discipline imposed from without, but who then imposes on himself a much more rigorous discipline from within.

Discipline simply means conquering one's self and bringing it under control so as to please God and live and work according to the code of conduct of an institution or profession. The importance of discipline in church leadership has been highlighted succinctly thus:

> Continual success cannot be achieved without discipline. Discipline is the basic set of tools we require to solve life's problems. Without discipline, we can solve nothing. With only some discipline we can solve only some problems. With total discipline, we can solve all problems. Some regard discipline as hardship. In reality, it permits success and sets you free from futile living. (Newman,1997:43).

The disciplined church leader or worker follows the narrow way of life. He does not live a carefree life. He controls himself and operations to be in line with the word of God, the constitution or bylaws of the church and the laws of the land. The apostle Paul writing about his life of discipline said:

> *Everyone who competes in the games goes into strict training. They do it to get a crown that will not last, but we do it to get a crown that will last forever. Therefore, I do not fight like a man beating the air. No, I beat my body and make it my slave so that after I have preached to others, I myself will not be disqualified for the prize (1 Cor.9:25-27).*

4.9. Humility

Church leaders and workers should understand that God has given them the privilege of serving his people. This does not mean that they have superior God-given knowledge. Leaders of God's people should therefore be dependent on God for understanding, power and fruitfulness. Concerning the virtue of humility, the scripture enjoins us thus:

> *Do nothing out of selfish ambition or vain conceit, but in humility consider others better than yourselves. Each of you should look not only to your own interest, but also to the interests of others. Your attitude should be the same as that of Christ Jesus: who being in the very nature of God did not consider equality with God something to be grasped but made himself nothing, taking the very nature of a servant, being made in human likeness. And being found in*

appearance as a man, he humbled himself and became obedient to death even the death of the cross (Philippians 2:3-7).

Leaders of God's people must learn to be humble for God resists the proud and gives grace to the humble (1 Peter 5:5). Leaders of God's people must take a cue from John the Baptist who said, "He must increase, but I must decrease. Lending support to the importance of humility in church leadership and ministry, Newman (90) observes:

> Humility is a very important characteristic in the life of a leader. Most people cannot stand folks who are full of themselves no matter what their successes are. However, true humility is appreciated by all. One of the surest signs of greatness is a humble spirit. The first test of a truly great person is their humility.

Church leaders who serve in pride instead of humility stand the risk of being rejected and humiliated by God and men. Humility, therefore, is a virtue to be imbibed by every church leader and worker.

4.10. Prudent Financial Management and Accountability

A servant leader is conscious of the fact that he is not the owner and the lord of the organization he leads. He is responsible to God and man, and consequently accountable to both. Consequently, he commits himself to prudent financial and other resource management, knowing that a one-day account will be required from him.

Prudent financial management expected of every church leader is characterised by the following:

a. Genuine, lawful and ethical sources of funds.
b. Careful spending of organizational money following the laid down guidelines.
c. Avoiding misappropriation and embezzlement of funds.

d. Keeping accurate and durable financial records.

   Highlighting the need for financial record keeping, Zimmerman (1995:524) maintains:

   The day is past when scraps of paper tacked away in some treasurer's pocket, suffice for financial records. Such haphazard methods are not only insufficient, they open the door to suspicion. Standard business practice not only guards funds but also protects reputation. The smaller church may find it difficult to get the expertise necessary to maintain a simple bookkeeping system. However, any intelligent person can follow a pattern, and simplified systems designed to this end which are furnished by the appropriate department in most denominational headquarters.

e. Budgeting and budget control. A Budget is the projected income and expenditure of an organization. It shows all the sources of income and how much is expected from each source. It also contains all the items of expenditure and how much is expected to be expended from each. A Budget should not be made for making sake. It should be controlled. Budgeting without budgetary control is a mere academic exercise. There should be budgetary control to avoid extra-budgetary expenditure and to ensure effective implementation.
f. Giving periodic financial reports or accounts and also after every major programme.

Emphasizing the need for accountability in leadership, Nwakaghinna (2013) maintains that once a person has accepted an appointment as a steward (trustee), he is bound by law to act in that capacity as the manager of the property, which is the subject of the trust to the beneficiaries. It is the cardinal duty of a trustee to provide accounts and information of the trust property and equally furnish necessary information as regards the same as may be required by the beneficiaries. It is incumbent on the trustee to keep accurate accounts of the trust property and furnish information about the same.

A responsible leader does not keep the people in the dark concerning the income and expenditure of the organization. Where necessary, periodic auditing is recommended. This will help to forestall the financial recklessness and abuses of some church leaders and workers.

CHAPTER 5

UNETHICAL (WRONG) MINISTERIAL CONDUCTS

In the introductory part of this work, it was pointed out that ethics deals with right and wrong conducts of man. Chapter four examined the right conduct expected of church ministers, leaders and workers. This chapter deals with the second part of ethics: the wrong conducts that are not expected of the church, workers. They are briefly examined.

5.1 Abuse:

Abuse has been explained as," the use of something in a way that is wrong or harmful" unfair, cruel or violent treatment of somebody" (Hornby, 2010: 6). Encarta Dictionary explains abuse with the following words:

Maltreatment: The physical psychological or sexual mistreatment of a person or animal.

Improper use: The illegal, improper or harmful use of something.

Improper practice: An illegal, improper or harmful practice.

Insults: Insulting or offensive language.

Abuse which can be classified as follows must be avoided by church leaders and workers:

- Child abuse
- Elder abuse
- Spousal (mate) abuse
- Physical abuse
- Psychological abuse
- Mental abuse
- Sexual abuse
- Scriptural abuse
- Drug abuse

Due to the fact that abuse is a burning ethical issue in our contemporary world and ministry, an attempt will be made to explain these abuses briefly.

Lending credence to this claim Collins (1988:294) maintains:

> Violence and abuse, especially in the home appears to be increasing. It is possible, of course that we are only now beginning to recognize the widespread prevalence of a problem that has been with us for centuries. Media attention and public outcries have riveted attention on child neglect and abuse, sexual violence, psychological maltreatment of children, rape, mates beating and mistreatment of the elderly. Various observers have confirmed that these problems of abuse not only are getting more attention, they are getting worse.

For the fact that abuses of different types are getting more attention and worse, necessity is laid on the author to briefly treat them.

Child Abuse: The U.S Child Abuse Prevention and Treatment Act defines child abuse as "physical or mental injury, sexual abuse or exploitation, negligent treatment or maltreatment of a child under the age of eighteen by a person who is responsible for the child's welfare and under circumstances which indicates the child's health or welfare, is harmed or threatened thereby (Martin, 1987:131).

Child abuse is an unethical behaviour that must be shunned by all church workers and leaders. There are different types of child abuse. They are briefly outlined below:

Physical abuse: This includes all kinds of deliberate act of violence that injure or kill a child. Sign of physical abuse on a child includes bruises, broken bones, burn marks etc.

Sexual Abuse: This occurs when an adult uses children for sexual gratification or expose them to sexual activities.

Emotional Abuse: This is the abuse that destroys a child's self-esteem. Such abuse commonly includes repeated verbal abuse in form of shouting, threats, humiliating, criticism, confining a child in a dark closet, social isolation by denying a child having friends, emotional neglect by not meeting the child's need for affection and comfort. Other emotional abuse to a child includes behaving in a cold and unaffectionate way towards a child, allowing a child to witness severe spousal abuse, the use of alcohol and drugs, encouraging juvenile delinquency, failure to meet a child's educational needs.

The causes of child abuse include, the mental disorders, intergenerational transmission of violence, social stress, social isolation and low community involvement and family structure. All this causes of child abuse should be avoided.
In Mark 10:13-16, Jesus was against child abuse. He spoke and acted against it. In that Scripture we read:

> *People were bringing little children to Jesus to have him touch them, but the disciples rebuked them. When Jesus saw this, he was indignant. He said to them, "Let the little children come to me, and do not hinder them, for the kingdom of God belongs to such as these. I tell you the truth; anyone who will not receive the kingdom of God like a little child will never enter it. And he took the children in his arms, put his hands on them and blessed them.*

Child abuse of any kind is unethical and must therefore be avoided by all church workers and parents. Hence the Apostle Paul enjoins: "Fathers, do not exasperate your children; instead, bring them up in the training and instruction of the Lord" (Ephesians :4).

Mate (spousal) Abuse: Most often than not, the wife is the victim of mate or spouse abuse. It includes deliberate physical assault, threats of violence, emotional abuse, forced sexual action, harshness, neglect and maltreatment.

Mate abuse is unethical and must be avoided by church leaders and workers. In the following scriptures, God condemns mate abuse in the strong words:

> *You ask "why", it is because the lord is acting as the witness between you and your wife of your youth because you have broken faith, though she is your partner, the wife of your marriage covenant…so guard yourself in your spirit and do not break faith with the wife of your youth. I hate divorce says the God of Israel, and I hate a man covering himself with violence as well as with his garment, says the lord Almighty. So guard yourself in your spirit and do not break faith (Malachi 2:14-16)*

Elder Abuse: This is the maltreatment of older people. It includes, rough handling like insult, beating, negligence, verbal condemnation, withholding of food, or medication, financial exploitation, deprivation of personal comfort and human contact.

Due to its unethical nature, God advised against elder abuse in 1Timothy 5:1 in these words, "Do not rebuke an older man harshly but exhort him as if he were your father"

Sexual Abuse: Sexual abuse can be experienced by children, teenagers, as well as adults. It can simply be explained as abnormal sexual activity. According to Collins (1988) sexual abuse includes exhibitionism, forced intercourse or other sexual behaviour which the victim resist, or foundling the sex organs of a minor or other person who is naive or powerless to resist.

Okeiyi (2012:16-37) enumerates the following as forms of sexual abuse: fornication, adultery, rape, prostitution, masturbation, homosexuality, incest, trans-sexualism, transvestitism, bestiality, pedophilia pedosexualism, necrophilia, fetishism, voyeurism, exhibition, masochism, orgies/group sex, sex charts, oral sex, non-genital sex, pornography and lust.

Included in sexual abuse is lesbianism. All form of sexual abuse is unethical and must never be tolerated by the church. Hence church workers and leaders should shun them.

Power Abuse: Scientifically speaking, power is the ability or capacity to do work. Spiritually speaking, it is the ability to cause a change in lives and situations of people though supernatural means. The British historian, Lord Action (1834-1902) once said "Power tends to corrupt and absolute power corrupts absolutely. Great men are almost always bad men.... There is no worse heresy than that the office sanctifies the holder of it". Writing against power abuse by leaders, William Shakespeare rightly observed that it is excellent to have a giant's strength but tyrannous to use it as a giant.

Church leaders have great powers conferred on them by God, men and the constitution and byelaws of their church. It is very much unethical for them to abuse powers conferred on them. Jezebel aided Ahab the king of Israel to abuse his Kingly power against Naboth in these words:

> *Get up and take possession of Naboth the Jezreelite that he refused to sell to you. He is no longer alive, but dead. Is this how you act as king over Israel, get up and eat! Cheer up. I will get you the vine yard of Naboth (1 Kings 21:7,15).*

Ahab abused his kingly power by killing Naboth and taking possession of his land. Power abuse by contemporary church leaders includes:

- Pronouncement of curses on people.
- Rash and unilateral suspension of disobedient members.
- Carting money away without due process of recording and accounting.

- Forcing members to labour for the leader at the expense of their welfare
- Using one's authority and position to take possession of what is not due to one.
- Meeting out corporal punishment on members.
- Unlawful, rash and unilateral removal of a person from office
- Acting contrary to the constitution and bye laws of an organization.
- Doing harm to people in any way.
- Wilfully denying people of their fundamental human rights.

People's fundamental human rights enumerated by Abaa (2001: 74-80) as provided in the Constitution of the Federal Republic of Nigeria includes:

- Right to life
- Right to personal liberty
- Right to fair hearing
- Right to private and family life
- Right to freedom of thought, conscience and religion
- Right to freedom of expression and press
- Right to peaceful assembly and association
- Right to freedom of movement
- Right to acquire and own immovable property anywhere in Nigeria

Scripture Abuse: The minister of the gospel is required of God to do proper exegesis of the scripture he presents to the people of God. Buttressing this point Ram (168) maintains: Exegesis is prior to any system of theology. The scriptures are themselves the divine disclosure. From them is derived our system of theology. We can only know the truth of God by correct exegesis of the scripture. Therefore, exegesis is prior to any system of theology. Great mischief has been done in the church when the system of theology or its framework has been derived extra biblically.

In order to avoid scripture abuse by teachers of the Bible, Jesus warned in Revelations 22:18, 19 that anybody who adds to the Bible what God has not said, God will add to him the plagues described in the book of Revelation. If anyone subtracts from the Bible, God will take away his share from the tree of life and in the holy city. Scripture abuse should be avoided by ministers of the gospel.

Spiritual Abuse: In the words of Johnson and Vanvonderen (1991:13), spiritual abuse occurs when people are treated in a way that damages or harms them spiritually as a result of which their relationship with God or the part of them capable of having relationship with God becomes wounded or scarred. When a person in need of help, support or greater spiritual empowerment is mistreated with result of weakening, undermining or decreasing that person's spiritual empowerment, spiritual abuse has occurred.
Actions that amount to spiritual abuse include the followings:

- Using spiritual power to dominate another person.
- Striking fear in a believer by use of spiritual power
- Keeping a Christian restless in performing religious activities with the notion that without so doing the person cannot be saved, win, succeed etc, thereby nullifying the grace of God.
- Tying a person to legalistic duties in order to get spiritual blessing or benefit.

Spiritual abuse should be avoided by spiritual leaders of the church. This is because it is subtly unethical.

5.2 Destructive Criticism

Encarta dictionary explains criticism as "a spoken or written opinion or judgement of what is wrong or bad about somebody or something; spoken or written opinions that point out one or more faults of somebody or something; judgment of or discussion about the qualities of something, especially a creative work".

Simply put, Criticism is finding fault with a persons' behaviour, action or work which can be expressed verbally or non-verbally. Writing on the place of criticism in servant leadership George Janvier and Bitrus Thaba (1997: 143) maintains:

> Criticism is inevitable and unavoidable in servant leadership. A servant leader must be prepared spiritually and emotionally to accept and respond to it. He should develop relationships with his critics so they would be free to come and air out their opinion to him.

The Criticism that is useful and recommended is constructive criticism which helps the leader to succeed. Leaders and all church workers should welcome constructive criticism as it is an ingredient for dynamic and successful leadership.

Destructive Criticism is unethical and must therefore be avoided by church workers and leaders. This is the criticism that attacks the person or the office of another leader with the view to pulling him down. Destructive Critics often hide themselves from their victims. They do not offer useful advice that will improve the work of the man they are trying to criticize. They are bent on destroying him thereby removing him from office. This type of criticism is unethical and ungodly. When Miriam and Aaron criticised Moses destructively because he married an Ethiopian woman, God rebuked them in these words:

When a prophet of the Lord is among you, I reveal myself to him in visions. I speak to him in dreams. But this is not true of my servant Moses; he is faithful in my house with him I speak face to face clearly and not in riddles; he sees the form of the Lord. Why then were you not afraid to speak against my servant Moses? (Numbers12:6-8).

Destructive criticism against a church leader is a serious sin in the sight of God. God did not rebuke Miriam and Aaron verbally; he punished Miriam with leprosy. Church leaders and workers should avoid destructive criticism of one another.

5.3 Wrong Communication Patterns

Communication is the art of transmitting information, ideas and attitudes from one person to another (Emery, Ault and Agee, 1971:3). Hessel-grave (1991:91) has rightly observed:

> The missionary task is fundamentally one of communication. In a very real sense, the missionary participates in the basic human change. While communication is an elemental human activity, it constitutes a fundamental human problem-perhaps second only the problems of his or her Adamic nature.

As has been pointed out above, the church leader or worker is a communicator. He communicates verbally and none verbally within and outside the church. Wrong (bad) communication is a problem of church leaders and workers that should be avoided. The scripture, James 3:2 buttresses the communicational problems the teachers of the word of God face in these words: "We all stumble in many ways. If anyone is never at fault in what he says, he is a perfect man, able to keep his whole body in check".

Wrong communication patterns church leaders and workers should avoid include the outlined below:

(a) Clear and present danger speeches: These are speeches that discourage people, incite people to riot, withdraw cooperation or over throw leadership.

(b) Speeches That Divulge Official Secret: These are speeches-formally or informally that divulge or reveal a secret matter discussed in a board meeting. This unethical behaviour has been causing problems at different levels of the church.

(c) Seducing Speech: The church leader should refrain from being a seducer in communication. Seduction is not just enticing somebody to sin. In gospel communication, a seducer is described by Griffin (1976:33-34) thus:

> The seducer uses deception and flattery to entice the other person into submission. He often appeals to irrelevant desires for success, money, popularity, or an easy life in order to accomplish his ends. He is willing to shade the truth because he fears the reality put a damper on the other person's response. The religious seducer is immoral because he maneuvers the listeners into making decision for the wrong reasons.

In communication of the word of God, the church leader should be open, truthful, plain and frank. He should not hide the severity of the claims of Christ for his disciples in order to win converts. He may do this by presenting only part of the gospel". The religious seducer's speech has the following characteristics:

1. Hiding the strict demands of the gospel for cross bearing and self-crucifixion.
2. Making bogus promises God has not made in the area of wealth acquisition, marriage, etc, to make the gospel attractive.
3. Offering people hope of prosperity without the conditionality of biblical principles of godliness, hard work and total obedience to the word of God.

(d) Speaking at The Audience: It has been posited by communicologists that the meaning of a speech resides with the audience. The Christian communicator should therefore avoid speaking at his audience for they will certainly assign meaning and understand the speech. Speaking at the audience means insulting the audience. Instead of being spoken at, the audience should be spoken to.

(e) A raping speech: A minister of the gospel should not be a rapist in carrying out his discipleship duty. Rape is obtaining something by force. A speech that forces people to accept religious idea is rape and is unethical. In the words of Griffin (1976:36) "the seducer, is immoral-we condemn him. The rapist is criminal-we remove him from the society".

The following words of Jesus to the apostles who went on missionary expedition is relevant here as it lends credence to the fact that rape in gospel communication is unethical. "But when you enter a town and are not welcomed, go into its streets and say; even the dust of your town that sticks to our feet we wipe off against you. Yet be sure of this; the kingdom of God is near" (Luke 10:10, 11).

Missionary history has it that Emperor Charlemagne was a rapist as he used rape to force Christianity on the Saxons. Kane (1982:42) reports the rape of Emperor Charlemagne (771-814) on the Saxons thus:

> The Savage Saxons wanted neither Christianity nor civilization. Both had to be imposed by force of arms, and in the process, atrocities were committed. On one occasion forty-five hundred Saxon men, woman and children were killed in one day by order of Charlemagne. Villages wee burned, crops were destroyed, whole communities wiped out all in an effort to impose Christian civilization on a pagan people. No wonder the missionaries won only but few converts.

5.4 Defamation of Character

This is also known as character assassination. This unethical behaviour is very rampant in the church. This is a deliberate and sustained attack on somebody's reputation. Defamation of character has been explained thus: The act of damaging the reputation of another by means of false and injurious communications that expose that person to contempt, ridicule, hatred, or social ostracism. In the common law, defamation in writing is classified as libel and oral defamation as slander (Microsoft Encarta premium, 2009).

A person's reputation determines the level a person can reach in life and in any vocation. It is an invaluable asset that should be jealously guarded. Consequently, an attack on a person's reputation is a direct attack on a person's life and destiny. It should therefore be avoided because of its unethical nature.

5.5 Rebellion

This is the attempt to overthrow the government/leadership or defiance of authority. Rebellion is one of the oldest sins in the world as it was generated by Lucifer with many angels joining him against God.

Rebellion at any level of church leadership and ministry is unethical and should therefore be shunned by church workers and leaders. In Numbers 16, Dathan and Korah with 250 princes of Israel rebelled against Moses and his leadership. God punished them by allowing the earth to swallow them up. This should serve as a deterrent to present- day members, workers and leaders of the church.

5.6 Causing Riots and Strike Actions

Riots and strike actions are strangers to Christianity and church ministry. In the secular world there is trade unionism. Therefore, riots and strike actions are often experienced where and when there are no industrial and relational harmony.

In criminal law, riot is an offence against the public peace. It is interpreted as any tumultuous disturbance by several persons who have unlawfully assembled to assist one another by the use of force if necessary against anyone opposing them in the execution of such enterprise in a violent manner to the terror of the people (Microsoft Encarta, 2009).

Strike actions are embarked upon by workers in Government and private company employments. It should not be so with those working for God in the church; no matter the sector of the church ministry they are involved in. In summary, riots and strike action are unethical behaviour in church life and ministry. Therefore, leaders must avoid them. This is because the church as the messianic community should be the signpost of the kingdom of God in the world.

5.7 Campaign and Politicking

Campaign and Politicking are twin and related actions of politicians with the aim of taking over or maintaining political position and power. Encarta dictionary explains campaign as "vote-seeking activities, e.g. rallies and speeches that are intended to persuade voters to vote a specific politician or party.

Campaign and politicking are unethical in Christian ministry and leadership. Absalom the son of David engaged in campaign and politicking against his father in order to overthrow him. The unethical behaviour of Absalom called Absalomism is reported in 2 Samuel 15:3-5 thus:

> Then Absalom would say to him, "look, your claims are valid and proper, but there is no representative of the king to hear you". And Absalom would add, "if only I were appointed a judge in the land, then everyone who has a complaint or case would come to me and I would see that he gets justice. Also, whenever anyone approaches him to bow down before him, Absalom would reach out his hand and take hold of him and kiss him. Absalom behaved in this way toward all the Israelites who came to the king asking for justice, and so he stole the hearts of all the men of Israel.

Absalom's campaign and politicking led to overthrowing his father and making himself king. The war that ensued led to his tragic end. Campaign and politicking are deadly both to individuals and to the church in general, they show be jettisoned.

5.8 Ministerial Trespass

Ministerial trespass has to do with encroachment or intrusion into another person's ministerial duties. As there is division of labour in economics and separation of powers in government, there is division of duty and power in church ministry. Trespass in the use of power and performance of duties is unethical.

An outstanding example of ministerial trespass is contained in the following scripture: *But after Uzziah became powerful his pride led to his downfall. He was unfaithful to the Lord his God and entered the temple of the Lord to burn incense on the altar of incense.... They confronted him and said, "It is not right for you Uzziah to burn incense to the Lord. That is for the priests, the descendants of Aaron...Uzziah, who*

> *had a censer in his hand ready to burn incense, became angry. While he was raging at the priests in their presence before the incense altar in the Lord's temple, leprosy broke out on his forehead (2 Chr.26:16-19).*

As we can see from the above, king Uzziah trespassed into the ministry of priests to offer sacrifice on the temple altar, he was a king not a priest. Pride did not allow him to listen to the eighty-one (81) priests who tried to dissuade him. God struck him with leprosy and he died as a leper.

In today's church, the clergy should mind their ministries and their oversight functions within the ambit of the law, the Bible, and the constitution and bye law of the church. Deacons, deaconesses and other church leaders and workers should not intrude into the work of the clergy.

5.9 Betrayal (Judasism)

Betrayal otherwise called Judasism in church ministry is highly unethical and satanic. Selling a person to another person or group of persons in order to kill him or destroy his name, image, ministry, leadership position etc, for selfish reasons is what is described as judasism. Judas betrayed his master, Jesus because of thirty pieces of silver (money). Today church leaders are betraying fellow church leaders. Church workers are betraying fellow church workers all because of earthly things that shall pass away. Betrayal is regarded as a great evil in the military, government and politics and in church ministry.

5.10 Sheep Stealing

This is the act of reconverting already Christians from one denomination or local church to one's denomination or local church through bad means. This practice is unethical and should be avoided by church leaders and workers. Buttressing on this point Schuller (2007:95) posits:

> If someone is already a Christian and active for the Lord, it is unpardonable sin to try to get him to leave, his church to come to yours. There are too many unbelievers to reach to waste time stealing members from other churches. Even if they are disgruntled with their church, you will be smart not to go after them. Often it would be a short time they are unhappy with you as well

5.11 Miscellaneous Unethical Conducts:

In the book: *Ministerial Ethics*: *Moral Formation for Church Leaders*, Joel E. Trull and James E. Carter enumerate unethical ministerial conducts. From the ideas enunciated in this book, the following points are added to the above list.

1. The minister not giving full service to his church as his primary assignment unless he is a part time pastor. If the minister is a full-time minister and decides to engage in extra-ministerial job may be to make ends meet, he must do that with the knowledge and approval of his

church leaders. He must not allow his extra-ministerial job encroach on his ministerial job and time.

2. Not making time for serious study in order to thoroughly comprehend, prepare and deliver his message, keep abreast of current thoughts and happenings, and develop his intellectual and spiritual capacities. It has been well said that reading makes a man. This is not truer in other vocations than in the church ministry. Church leaders are expected of God and men to be readers. This necessitated this injunction to Bishop Timothy: " Study to show thyself approved unto God, a workman that needeth not to be ashamed, rightly dividing the word of truth" (2 Timothy 2:15)
3. Making his remuneration primary and his service secondary. The church ministerial job is not a secular job where there is bargain for salary. The church worker should therefore make his service primary and his remuneration secondary. The church worker's job has eternal reward therefore, he should not base his service on the amount of remuneration he receives. God knows how to pay his workers.
4. Not taking care of one's health so as to be physically fit.
5. Over working one's self when there are assistants to help do the work due to selfishness.
6. Telling lies or half-truth in order to convince your audience.
7. Being guilty of plagiarism. This is using another person's sermon material or intellectual property without acknowledging the source.
8. Falling into debts due to financial indiscipline.
9. Bringing reproach to the church by joining improper persons in marriage.
10. Breaking contracts and agreements made with the church.
11. Engaging in other remunerative work without the knowledge and consent of the leaders of the work.
12. Divulging confidential information given by members without their consent.
13. Taking sides with factions in the church.
14. Interfering directly or indirectly with the work of another pastor.

15. Rendering some ministerial services to the members of another pastor without consulting him except in the case of emergencies.
16. Making overtures from a church whose pastor is still serving.
17. Speaking ill of the character or the work of another pastor, your predecessor of successor.
18. Leaving a station with an official property.
19. Continuously visiting a station you served and left even without the consent of the incumbent pastor.
20. Leaving the parsonage and premises in other than good condition.
21. Ministerial jealousy (especially where there are many ministers).

CHAPTER 6

ETHICAL SOCIAL ISSUES AND CHURCH MINISTRY

The ministry of the church is all about human life as it touches all the facets of life. This is predicated on the fact that Jesus our example says "The thief comes only to steal and kill and destroy; I have come that they may have life, and have it to the full" (John10:10).

Ethical issues to be examined in this chapter are issues of life which have to do with allowing or not allowing human life to be lived to the full. These ethical life issues include abortion, suicide, assisted suicide, euthanasia, divorce and remarriage. As the church serves humanity through medical missions, counselling, etc. church workers may come face to face with the above issues. They are hereby examined in the light of biblical Christian ethics.

6.1 ABORTION

Abortion is a household social issue in our contemporary society. It has been described as the termination of a pregnancy before birth resulting in the death of the fetus (Redmond, 2009:1). Abortion is classified into two: natural (spontaneous) and induced abortion:

Natural (spontaneous) Abortion:

Natural or spontaneous abortion is also called miscarriage. This may occur due to the following reasons: the foetus not developing normally, the pregnant woman having an injury or disorder that prevents her from carrying the pregnancy to the end by delivering the child. As miscarriage is not an intentional act, the victim has no case to answer for its occurrence.

Induced Abortion:

This is the abortion that is intentionally carried out. Some reasons adduced for induced abortion include:

- Unwanted pregnancy
- Pregnancy which presents a risk to the woman's health.
- Foetus having potential physical or mental problems when born.

Induced abortion is the focus of debates in the world today which has generated polarizing ethical and philosophical issues. The author here intends to point out the unethical nature of induced abortion so that church workers and Christians should avoid and condemn it.

The abortion debate has divided people into two camps namely, the pro-choice supporters and the pro-life advocates. The pro-choice supporters maintain that a woman has reproductive rights and should be allowed to exercise it even the right to choose to have an abortion. Pro-life advocates oppose abortion for any reason unless when the mother's life is threatened by carrying the pregnancy or a logical conclusion. The arguments of the pro-choice supporters and pro-life advocates are succinctly summed thus: At one end of this ethical spectrum are pro-choice defenders who believe, that the fetus is only a potential human being until when it becomes viable, that is able to survive outside its mother's womb. Until this time, the fetus has no legal rights i.e. the rights belong to the woman carrying the fetus, who can decide whether or not to bring the pregnancy to full term. At the other end of the spectrum are pro-life supporters who believe the fetus is a human being from the time of conception. As such, the fetus has the legal right to life from the moment the egg and sperm unite (McGee Merz, 2009:1).

Both the pro-choice supporters and pro-life advocates have their supporters which have generated hot debates for and against abortion, leaving a continuum of ethical religious, philosophical and political positions. This work pitches tent with the pro-life advocates to condemn abortion as unethical, unchristian and ungodly. It must therefore be avoided by all Christians. This is because actual human life begins in the womb as soon as the fetus is formed. This has biblical backing as we see in the following Scripture: "The word of the Lord came to me saying, "Before I formed you in the womb I know you, before you were born, I set you apart; I appointed you as a prophet to the nations" (Jeremiah 1:4, 5).

God the creator of man recognized Jeremiah as a human being when he was still in the womb as a fetus. God set him apart for prophetic ministry even in the womb. If God recognized Jeremiah as a human being in the womb, he recognizes every other fetus in the womb of a woman as a human being. Nobody therefore has the right to terminate human life in the womb through induced abortion.

From the ongoing, it can be understood that two questions are involved in the abortion debate. These are biological and philosophical/ theological questions. The biological question asks, "At what stage and where does the individual life of an offspring begin? Biological facts make it clear that from conception till birth, the foetus is a living, human individual demarcated from the parents.
The philosophical question asks, "Is the foetus which the science of biology says is a human being from conception to be regarded as a person?" Isaramen (180) maintains that the clearest extreme position which denies some personality to some individuals is that which treats the person as a function of society. Montangu (1965:12) was of this extreme position when he said, "The embryo, foetus and newborn of the human species, in point of fact, do not really become functionally human until humanized in the human socialization process. Humanity is an achievement, not an endowment".

This principle of genuine human realization (activation) adopted by Montangu opens the way not only for abortion but also for infanticide. In response to this theory, it has been argued that since the embryo develops by interaction with the material organs, socialization with most fundamental modes of biological communication has taken place. If humanity is determined in terms of achievement, does it mean that those who have made no achievement are not humans? What do we do with those without potentiality or those whose potentiality has been impaired like the handicapped or de-formed? Are we to kill them or not to care for them?

Theologically or biblically speaking, using the principle of genuine human realization to commit abortion is evil and God will certainly judge the perpetrators. From the Bible, we learn that we should love, cherish, care and protect the weak, the defenceless, the unwanted, and the handicapped.

In Genesis 9:5&6 God says:

> And for your lifeblood, I will surely demand an accounting. I will demand an accounting from every animal. And from each man too, I will demand an accounting for the life of his fellow man. Whoever sheds the blood of man, by man shall his blood be shed for in the image of God has God made man.

As a conclusion to this section, we restate that the foetus in the womb of a woman became a living human being from the time of conception. Its socialization also starts in the womb and continues after birth. Therefore, to eliminate an unwanted pregnancy is to shed human blood. As can be seen from the above scripture, God will judge those who take human life either through abortion or other means. The church in its ministry to the world must speak against abortion and avoid it in its medical services to society.

Many Western countries have legalized abortion for different reasons. In the United States of America, the legalization of abortion started in 1996 when the State of Mississippi passed a law permitting abortion in cases of rape. Other reasons for which abortion has been legalized in the States include- a threat to a woman's health, pregnancy resulting from incest, the foetus having serious abnormalities, and pregnancy of girls under 18 years of age. The effect of the legalization of abortion is an increase in the abortion rate as the data below shows.

Number and ratio of Legal Abortions in the U.S.A

YEAR	LEGAL ABORTIONS	RATIO
1975	1034000	331
1979	1498000	420
1980	1554000	428
1981	1577000	430
1982	1574000	428
1983	1575000	436
1984	1577000	423
1985	1589000	422
1986	1574000	416
1987	1559000	405
1988	1591000	401
1989	1567000	380
1990	1609000	389
1991	1557000	379
1992	1529000	380
1993	1500000	378
1994	1431000	364
1995	1364000	351
1996	1366000	351
1997	1335000	341
1998	1319000	334
1999	1315000	327

Source: Microsoft Encarta Premium, 2009.

Comparative Rates of Abortion
Abortion Rate Per 1,000 women age 15 – 44

Country	Year	Reporting
Albania	1996	27.2

Armenia	1996	35.4
Australia	1995-96	22.2
Azerbaijan	1996	16.0
Bangladesh	1995-96	3.8
Belarus	1996	67.5
Belgium[1]	1996	6.8
Bulgaria	1996	51.3
Canada[2]	1995	15.5
Croatia	1996	12.9
Cuba	1996	77.7
Czech Republic	1996	20.7
Denmark	1995	16.1
Estonia	1996	53.8
Finland	1996	9.9
France	1995	12.4
FYROM[3]	1996	28.5
Georgia	1996	21.9
Germany	1996	7.6
Hungary	1996	34.7
India	1995-96	2.7
Ireland[4]	1996	5.9
Israel	1995	14.3
Italy	1996	11.
an	1995	13.4
zakhstan	1996	43.9
gyzstan	6	4
via	6	1
uania	6	4
dova	6	3
ngolia	6	9
Netherlands	6	
v Zealand	5	4
way	6	6
nania	6	0
ssia	5	4

gapore	16	9
vakia	16	7
venia	16	8
ıth Africa	17	
ıth Korea[6]	16	6
ıin	16	
əden	16	7
tzerland[7]	16	
kistan[8]	10	1
ıisia	16	
key[9]	13	0
aine	16	3
ted States	16	9
ɔekistan	16	3
tnam[10]	16	3

rosoft ® Encarta ® 2009. © 1

6.2 EUTHANASIA

The term, "euthanasia" has been defined in different ways by many scholars, health personnels and health associations. According to Rose (1912:598), euthanasia may be defined "as the doctrine or theory that in certain circumstances when owing to disease, senility, or the like, a person's life has permanently ceased to be either agreeable or useful, tho sufferer should be painlessly killed, either by himself or by another" Simply put, euthanasia is the practice of mercifully ending a person's life in order to release the person from an incurable disease, intolerable suffering or undignified death. Euthanasia is the Greek word meaning "good death" which originally referred to intentional merciful killing.

Due to medical advances made in prolonging the lives of dying or comatose patients, euthanasia also applies to lack of action to prevent death. Euthanasia can be described as being:

- Active
- Passive
- Voluntary
- Involuntary

Active Euthanasia: Euthanasia can be active when an individual is painlessly put to death for merciful reasons; for instance, when a doctor administers a lethal dose of medication to a patient.

Passive Euthanasia: This involves doing nothing to prevent death; for instance, when a doctor refrains from using an artificial respirator to sustain the life of a terminally-ill patient.

Voluntary Euthanasia: In voluntary Euthanasia, a person willingly and voluntarily asks to die and is therefore made to die.

Involuntary Euthanasia: This refers to ending the life of a person who is not mentally competent to make an informed request to die; such as a patient in comatose.

Historical Background of Euthanasia

Euthanasia has existed and has been accepted in some forms in history. In ancient Greece and Rome, helping people to die or putting them to death was permitted under certain conditions. In the Greek city of Sparta, babies born with several defects were put to death. Voluntary Euthanasia for elderly persons was an accepted custom in many ancient societies (Redmond,2008).

As Christianity grew and spread in the West, euthanasia became morally and ethically bad and was viewed as a violation of God's gift of life. A contemporary branch of Christianity, Judaism and Islam condemn active euthanasia, although some permit restricted forms of passive euthanasia.

Explaining the legality or otherwise of euthanasia Tom (2008) posits:

> Following traditional religious principles, western laws have generally treated the act of assisting someone in dying as a form of punishable homicide (unlawful killing). However, in modern times laws have become secular. Those who wish to legalize euthanasia have argued that under principles of individual liberty (such as those expressed in the Constitution of the United States), individuals have the legal right to die as they choose. Most countries (including the United States) have not fully adopted this position and retain restrictions on euthanasia.

The pertinent question to ask here is," Is it morally right for a church worker to be involved in active or passive euthanasia? In dealing with this question Onimhawo (1998:9) maintains:

> The moral issues involved in active and passive (killing and letting die) euthanasia have been quite controversial. Some scholars do not see any difference between active and passive euthanasia, because, for them, there is no general moral difference between killing and letting die. Some scholars, however, believe that there is a difference between active and passive euthanasia. These scholars argue that active euthanasia involves killing someone. But passive euthanasia merely involves letting someone die, and while morally permissible, others argue that, though killing and letting die may be morally permissible, in certain circumstances, our obligation to refrain from killing is more binding than our obligation not to let others die.

In as much as the moral difference between active and passive euthanasia is minimal, the difference is significant. This is because moral distinctions are very crucial when human life is involved.

In dealing with the question of the morality of euthanasia-whether passive or active or passive, Marx (1985:14) succinctly puts his argument thus:

> The morality of any act (whether one of commission or omission) depends on what is intended as well as what is done (or not done). It is a mistake to assume that, in the context of euthanasia, "active" and "passive" refer to physical activity alone. Just as "pulling the plug" is not active euthanasia unless one's intention is to kill, so too the physical passivity of doing nothing at all can be an act of murder. Morally speaking, an injured man who idly watches himself bleed to death without trying to stop the bleeding is guilty of suicide as if he had inflicted the injury himself. Where a lethal motive is present, physical "passivity" cannot be justified as "letting nature take its course"

In conclusion to this section, it is necessary to point out that from the teachings of the Holy Bible, the word of God, euthanasia is unbiblical and immoral. The Bible condemns taking human life whether by act of commission or omission (Exodus 20:13) The church in the course of providing medical services to the people of the world as part of her missionary enterprise, euthanasia of all types should be avoided because it is unethical.

6.3 Assisted Suicide

Assisted suicide is a person's voluntary suicide with the help of another individual. Assisted suicide also refers to the act of providing an individual with the means to commit suicide, knowing that the recipient plans to use the means to end his or her own life. If a doctor provides medications or other means of committing suicide with the understanding that a patient may intentionally use them to end his or her own life, this act is known as physician-assisted suicide (Beauchamp, 2008).

Assisted suicide can be carried out in the following ways:

i. When a person facing acute illness or extreme physical suffering refuses treatment offered by doctors.
ii. When a person in danger of death refuses to accept rescue help e.g. a drowning person refusing to be rescued.

It is widely held that those who commit suicide with a doctor's assistance are different category from those who simply refuse.

The ethical issue regarding assisted suicide is whether acts by doctors who help others kill themselves (or let others die) are morally right. Those who believe that assisted suicide is morally wrong maintain that it is impermissible for a doctor to kill a person. There is a distinction between killing a person and letting a person die. Supporters of assisted suicide argue that its rightness or wrongness depends on the justification underlying the action.

Medical ethicists agree that physicians may forgo treatment when a person or patient-authorized representative refuses treatment. However, the traditional view in professional medical ethics is that a request for assistance in dying does not justify an action of physician-assisted suicide.

From the biblical point of view, assisted suicide is unethical whether there is a valid request for it by a patient or his/her authorized representatives.

6.4 Same-Sex Marriage

Same-sex marriage otherwise called gay marriage is another ethical issue that deserves discussion in this section. It has recently been a debated ethical issue that has attracted the attention of world political and religious leaders. The people involved in same-sex marriage are either homosexuals or lesbians.

The ethical issue involving same-sex marriage seeks to ascertain the ethical soundness or otherwise of gay marriage. Should the church wed and accommodate the gay people in the discharge of her missionary duties? Members of the international community and the church are divided over this issue. In the Daily Sun of Friday 31, 2014 the Archbishop of Canterbury and York were reported as writing a letter to the President of Nigeria and Uganda about laws penalising gay people. According to the said letter, homosexual people were loved and valued by God and should not be victimized or diminished. In their letter, the archbishop reiterated their support for the document "Dromantine Communiqué published in 2005 by the primates of the Anglican communion. The communiqué says:

> We continue unreservedly to be committed to the pastoral support and care of homosexual people. The victimization or dismastment of human beings whose affection happens to be ordered towards people of the same sex is anathema to us. We assure homosexual people that they are children of God, loved and valued by Him and deserving of the best we can give pastoral care and friendship.

From the above, it is clear that the Bishop of Canterbury, Justin Webby and Arch. Bishop John Sentami of York is in support of homosexuality. The United Nations Human Rights Chief Navy described the Nigerian law forbidding same-sex marriage as "draconian". She said that she had rarely seen a law that in so few paragraphs directly violates so many basic universal human rights.

Gay marriage is against natural and divine laws that regulate marital and sexual relationships. The city of Sodom and Gomorrah was noted for homosexuality and other kinds of sexual perversions. Sodomites in Sodom and Gomorrah attracted God's wrath and judgement which led to the city with its inhabitants being destroyed with fire.
Concerning this event the Scripture records:

> *Before they had gone to bed, all the men from every part of Sodom-both young and old- surrounded the house. They called to Lot, "Where are the men who came to you tonight? Bring them out to us so that we can have sex with them. And the angels who did not*

keep their positions of authority but abandoned their own home-these he has kept in darkness, bound with everlasting chains for judgement on the great day. In a similar way, Sodom and Gomorrah and the surrounding towns gave themselves up to sexual immorality and perversion. They serve as an example of those who suffer the punishment of eternal fire (Gen.4:4,5; Jude:7).

The way God judged and punished Sodom and Gomorrah is a clear indication that God is against all forms of sexual perversions like homosexuality, lesbianism, and gay marriage. Those who despise the counsel of God and go into same-sex sexual relationships and marriage are going contrary to God's word.

In Leviticus 18:22 God commanded his covenant people, Israel, "Do not lie with a man as one lies with a woman; that is detestable. This is a divine injunction against homosexuality and invariably against lesbianism and gay marriage. The punishment for homosexuals in the Old Testament is stated in Leviticus 20:13 thus: "If a man lies with a man as one lies with a woman, both of them have done what is detestable. They must be put to death; their blood will be on their own heads". The death punishment attached to gay living depicts the seriousness of this sin in the eyes of the Holy God. Homosexuality is among the wicked immoral acts whose practitioners will never inherit the kingdom of God. This is succinctly stated in 1 Corinthians 6:9, 10 thus: *Do you not know that the wicked will not inherit the kingdom of God? Do not be deceived. neither the sexually immoral nor idolaters nor adulterers nor male prostitutes nor homosexual offenders nor thieves nor the greedy nor drunkards nor slanderers nor swindlers will inherit the kingdom of God.*

From the above Scriptures, it is crystal clear that God views gay life and gay marriage with great seriousness as wickedness against God. It should therefore be entirely discouraged by all church leaders and workers. Church leaders should not join gay people as husbands and wives.

Furthermore, gay people should not be ordained as ministers of the gospel or as church leaders and workers.

6.5 Divorce and Remarriage

Some Pharisees came to Jesus to test him. They asked, "Is it lawful for a man to divorce his wife for any and every reason?" "Haven't you read" he replied, "that at the beginning the Creator made them male and female and said, for this reason, a man will leave his father and mother and be united to his wife and the two will become one flesh. So, they are no longer two but one; Therefore, what God has joined together, let no man separate (Matt. 19:3-6).

Marriage is the oldest institution in the world. God himself instituted marriage and laid its foundation. The sanctity of marriage is grounded on the authority of God himself. Divorce occasioned by human selfishness is the devil's greatest arsenal against the marriage institution. Divorce is a socio-religious problem that has a multiplier negative effect on the society. Cases of divorce and remarriage are becoming rampant and are growing to an alarming proportion every day. This problem is rampant among Christians and non-Christians. Newspapers, court reports and church minutes are replete with marital cases bothering or divorce and remarriages.

It has therefore become necessary to examine this problem in a book of this nature. This will help us know whether the church and its leaders should allow divorce and remarriage or not. It is necessary to state inter alia that God is against divorce for it is totally against his intention for marriage. This assertion is buttressed in Jesus' statement above "*Therefore what God has joined together let no man separate*" (Matt. 19:6). God's abhorrence of divorce is also made plain in the following statement to Israelites through the prophet Malachi:

> *Has not the Lord made them one? In flesh and spirit, they are his. And why one? Because he was seeking a godly offspring. So, guard*

yourself in your spirit and do not break faith with the wife of your youth. I hate divorce says the LORD GOD of Israel, "and I hate a man's covering himself with violence as well as with his garment", says the Lord Almighty, so guard yourself in your spirit and do not break faith (Mal 2:15-16).

God says loud and clear, "I hate divorce". The church should hate what God hates. Christians also should hate what God hates and reject divorce at all cost.

According to Collins (1988:451), The difficulties of marriage and the pains of divorce have led some compassionate Christians to reinterpret or deemphasize biblical teachings in an effort to make divorce and remarriage seem easier and more acceptable. Ignoring or deemphasizing biblical teaching is neither compassionate nor helpful. If we are to be effective, Christian counsellors must have a clear understanding of the scriptural statements about divorce and remarriage.
Collins enumerates four schools of thought and understandings on biblical teaching about divorce, they are as follows:

1. Those who conclude that marriage is for life, and that divorce is never permitted on biblical grounds, and that remarriage of a divorced person always is adultery.
2. Those who conclude that there are legitimate biblical grounds for divorce and that remarriage is permitted under these circumstances.
3. Those who maintain that when circumstances arise that defy solution, divorce becomes necessary for the sake of the mental, emotional or physical health of the spouses or their children. This is based on general biblical principles rather than any specific biblical teaching.
4. Those who hold to the view that the church or court can annul marriage and make way for remarriage.

Old Testament Teaching on Divorce

The Bible clearly teaches that marriage is permanent and that there should be no divorce. Due to the fall of man which has made humans to live on sub ideal level, God permitted divorce and gave guidelines for it. This practice is tolerated but is never commanded or divinely encouraged. In Deuteronomy 24:1-2, the Scripture says:

> *When a man hath taken a wife, and married her, and it comes to pass that she finds no favour in his eyes because he hath found uncleanliness in her; then let him write her a bill of divorcement and give it in her hand, and send her out of his house. And when she is departed out of his house, she may go and be another man's wife. (KJV).*

According to the above Old Testament scripture, divorce was to be legal with a written document or certificate of divorcement given to the woman and permissible only when uncleanliness was involved. Unfortunately, the meaning of "uncleanliness" has become a subject of debate. Concerning the interpretation of "uncleanliness" as a ground for divorce there are two disputing and opposing schools of thought: These are schools of Shammai and Hillel.

According to Shammai, "Something indecent" or "Uncleanliness" meant "Marital unfaithfulness" as the only allowable cause for divorce. For Hillel, a man could divorce his wife if she did anything he disliked even if she burnt his food while cooking. Jesus took sides with Shammai when he said "But I tell you that anyone who divorces his wife, except for marital unfaithfulness, causes her to become an adulteress" (Matt. 5:32). The Greek word for unfaithfulness is 'porneia' which refers to all sexual relationships outside marriage.

Extramarital sex violates the one flesh concept that is basic to Biblical marriage. On this issue, Collins (452) maintains:

> Even when unfaithfulness is involved, divorce is not commanded. It is merely permitted. Forgiveness and reconciliation still are preferable to divorce. Nevertheless, if divorce does occur under these circumstances, it is the opinion of many evangelical biblical scholars that the innocent party is free to remarry.

It is the author's opinion that a one-time action of marital unfaithfulness is not enough grounds for divorce. The offended party should forgive. It is only when the marital unfaithfulness becomes habitual that the cheated spouse may seek divorce and remarriage.

The Teachings of Paul on Divorce and Remarriage:
In his teaching on marriage, divorce and remarriage, the Apostle Paul maintained:

> *To the married, I give this command (not I, but the Lord): A wife must not separate from her husband. But if she does, she must remain unmarried or else be reconciled to her husband. And a husband must not divorce his wife. To the rest I say this (I, not the Lord) if any brother has a wife who is not a believer and she is willing to live with him, he must not divorce her. And if a woman has a husband who is not a believer and he is willing to live with her, she must not divorce him...But if the unbeliever leaves, let him do so. A believing man or woman is not bound in such circumstances; God has called us to live in peace. (1 Cor. 7:10-15).*

In the above scripture, the Apostle Paul reechoed Christ's teaching on the permanence of marriage. He however added the second reason for divorce, namely desertion by an unbelieving spouse. In the case of desertion by the unbelieving mate, St. Paul maintains that the deserted partner is not bound to remain single. In other words, he or she is free to remarry.

Causes of Divorce

- Collins enumerates causes of divorce as Sexual unfaithfulness
- Desertion by an unbelieving spouse
- Escalating incompatibility
- Social sanctions
- Immature attitudes
- Persisting stresses

On the above and other causes of marriage divorce, Collins (454) maintains:

> There is no one cause of divorce. Every marriage is different, and each divorce comes because of a unique combination of causes and circumstances. When these problems are not resolved divorce is more likely. The following influences sometimes motivate one or both of the spouses to initiate divorce action.

1. **Sexual Unfaithfulness:** Infidelity has been described as the most common disruptive force in families, the most devastating and the most universally accepted justification for divorce. Infidelity should be avoided for even when it is confessed and discussed with one's partner, the marriage is likely to be negatively jeopardized. Although from a biblical standpoint, divorce is permitted for the reason of sexual unfaithfulness, forgiveness and reconciliation are to be preferred to divorce. This is because as somebody has suggested, no one wins in a divorce. Everybody loses- the couple, their children, their parents, and the community at large.
2. **Desertion:** To the teaching of Jesus on the indissolubility of marriage except for the case of sexual unfaithfulness, Paul added desertion as a second legitimate reason for divorce. According to Saint Paul in 1 Corinthians 7:10-15, when an unbelieving spouse leaves, the believer is free to remarry.

   If the departed partner has been involved in sexual unfaithfulness or if the departure has been so long that there is no hope of reconciliation, then in the words of Ellison (1977:58):

> A *defacto* divorce will have taken place, whether or not it has been sought or granted... Although God's desire is always for reconciliation where that is impossible because of the partner's recalcitrance, there is no useful purpose served in refusing to acknowledge dissolution. Desertion in that sense becomes divorce.

In the light of the aforesaid, a departure by an unbelieving partner which is impossible to reconcile can be a ground for divorce and remarriage.

Other Causes of divorce include escalating incompatibility, social sanctions, immature attitudes, and persistent stresses that are not supported by the Bible. They will therefore not be discussed in this section.

Sequel to the fact that divorce has emotional, behavioural, social, and spiritual effects, it should be prevented. The permanence and sanctity of marriage should be maintained.

Church leaders and workers should therefore not grant divorce and remarriage on demand except in conformity with biblical reasons for divorce and remarriage. Ministers of the gospel should seek for the reconciliation of deserted spouses.

CHAPTER 7

MINISTERIAL ETIQUETE, PROTOCOL AND COURTESY

7.1. Definitions: For a proper understanding of the subject matters of this chapter namely, etiquette, protocol and courtesy in the Christian ministry, it is pertinent to define each of them.

a. **Etiquette:** The Oxford English Dictionary defines the word "etiquette" as "the customary code of polite behaviour in society or among members of a particular profession or group". Ministerial etiquette therefore is the normative polite behavior expected of those involved in Christian service.

b. **Protocol:** According to the Oxford English Dictionary, protocol is "the official procedure or system of rules governing affairs of a state or diplomatic occasions". It is the accepted or established code of procedure or behaviour in any group, organization or situation.

c. **Courtesy:** This is the showing of politeness and respect in one's attitude and behaviour towards others.

The importance of etiquette, protocol and courtesy in any vocation cannot be over-emphasized as they ensure peaceful and harmonious relationships in every organization. The God we serve is the God of orderliness. Therefore orderliness, peaceful and harmonious relationships should characterize Church and parachurch ministries. Every minister of the gospel should observe ministerial etiquette, protocol and courtesy in order to succeed.

7.2. Ministerial Etiquette: Ministerial etiquette helps us to know how to treat others respectfully and appropriately in any context which will foster meaningful relationships and create a comfortable and relaxed atmosphere wherever we serve. A minister of the gospel is involved in five types of business etiquettes as listed in http:/blog.hubspot.com:

- Workplace etiquette
- Table manners and meal etiquette
- Professional etiquette
- Communication etiquette
- Meetings etiquette

Rules of ministerial etiquette include, but are not limited to the following:

- Showing up on time in meetings and programmes.
- Being considerate of people around you.
- Refrain from gossiping about fellow ministers.
- Avoid interrupting others in their ministries directly or indirectly.
- Dressing appropriately and respectfully.
- Avoid being on your phone when a Church programme is going on.
- Checking your emails, sms, WhatsApp, etc messages and replying on time.
- Avoid eating at the wrong places like open places and along the road.
- Try not to call unannounced
- Try to remember people's names
- Greeting people
- Always knocking before entering people's houses or office
- Showing respect to people
- Being yourself
- Always say “thank you”, “I am sorry”, and “please” when necessary.
- Give genuine compliments
- Do not be boastful or arrogant
- Listen before speaking
- Speak with kindness and caution
- Do not criticize destructively
- Maintain eye contact
- Smile when necessary

7.3. Ministerial Protocol: Ministerial protocol is basically how ministers should conduct themselves in the worship and service of God. The essence of ministerial protocol is to maintain orderliness and decency in the worship of God and in the ministry. According to Boyd, the Church is the most important place where dignity, protocol, respect and reverence should be maintained. In http/www.sermoncentral.com Protocol is described thus:

> The term protocol carries from the Greek words meaning "the first glue". Nowadays, protocol can be understood as the glue which holds official life in the society together. Whether on the local, national or international level, proper protocol is vital in assuring the relations between the officials of organizations and governments are conducted with maximum efficiency. Protocol is defined as a system of rules and acceptable behaviour used at official ceremonies and occasions or a code of ceremonial forms and courtesies of procedures accepted as proper and correct in official dealing.... Protocol should be followed because God is not the author of confusion but of peace in the Church.

Ministerial protocol involves the following but is not limited to:

- Catering for the well-being of the pastor and facilitating his ministry by providing requisite support services to assist his ministry without hindrance.
- Attending all required meetings and services
- Following the routine duties according to the fundamental principles laid down by the church
- Providing protocol services for guest speakers
- Identifying ministers and other guests and according them proper recognition
- Following the laid down formalities during special meetings
- Following the laid down procedure in the introduction of guests: knowing where to begin and stop for another person to take over.

- Taking care of guest ministers and attending to all logistics in relation to their visit
- Being polite and helpful to fellow ministers
- Having preliminary engagement with a guest speaker prior to his arrival in order to seek information about his needs during the visit. Such needs may include transportation, accommodation, feeding etc.
- Ensuring that when visiting a Church or attending an occasion you do not occupy a seat meant for those higher than you in the ministry (Luke 14:8-11).

7.4. Ministerial Courtesy:

Courtesy has been defined at the beginning of this chapter as the showing of politeness and respect in one's attitude and behaviour towards others. The importance of courtesy in every profession cannot be over-emphasized.

Highlighting the value of courtesy in the Christian service, Catherine Evaritt-Newton posited:

> Courtesy is one of the graces of the spirit and should be cultivated by all. It has the power to soften men and things. Without it, things could become hard and rough. Those who profess to be followers of Christ and are at the same time rough, unkind and uncourteous have not learned Jesus.

The following constitute ministerial courtesy as enumerated by Catherine Everitt-Newton:

- Having respect for the ministries and pulpits of others
- Staying out of the internal affairs of other Churches
- Not perceiving another minister as a threat
- Holding the door for another person
- Expression of gratitude for work done – Listening before offering your opinion
- Greeting people properly

- Introducing yourself to people who do not know you before dealing with them
- Responding to every invitation you receive whether your answer is yes or no.
- Remembering and using people's names.
- Not assuming that others have time to answer your queries, thereby always asking: “May I interrupt you? etc.”
- Dressing properly and appropriately
- Being punctual in meetings, occasions and programmes
- Avoiding operating the handphone when preaching is going on or when conversing with someone

Other courteous behaviours expected of ministers of the gospel include, but are not limited to the following:

- Crediting the owner of any intellectual property you borrowed (avoiding plagiarism)
- Not being in competition with any minister in the ministry of the word of God
- Refusing to speak disrespectfully about the work of predecessor or successor
- Refraining from visiting your former station or still influencing the members of your former station to the detriment of the ministry of your successor.
- Notifying the minister in charge of your former station should there arise a need for you to visit
- Giving recognition to your associate ministers or co-leaders publicly
- Avoiding suppression of your associate minister
- Accepting responsibility for what goes wrong in your domain
- Keeping to the time allotted to you in your ministration as a guest speaker.
- Avoid closing your eyes or looking away when a sermon is going on.

- Except when it is absolutely necessary do not go out when a message is ongoing only to return after the message.
- Avoid displaying I know-it-all attitude when preaching or teaching is going on.
- As a guest speaker, avoid collecting the contacts of the members of the Church where you are visiting.

As a conclusion to this chapter, it is worthy of note that ministerial ethics must go in pari-passu with ministerial etiquette, protocol and courtesy. All ministers of the gospel, Church leaders and indeed all Church workers must be committed to them. They are desiderata for acceptable and successful Christian service. Those who are committed to them will at the end receive our Lord's commendation, "Well done, good and faithful servant" (Matthew 25:21).

BIBLIOGRAPHY

Abba, J.J. (2001).Law *for the Lay Man*. Abuja: Olu Prints Nig. Ltd.

Claebaut , D.D.(1983).*Urban Ministry*. Grand Rapids, Michigan: Zondevan Publishing House.

Dayton, E.R. and Fraser, D.A. (1990). *Planning Strategies for World Evangelization*. Grand Rapids, Michigan: Williams B. Eerdmans Publishing Company.

Emery, E. and Others *(1997)*. *Introduction to Mass Communication*. New York: Dodd.

Emory, A.G. (1987). *The Art of Christian Persuasion*. Wheaton, Illinois: Tyndale House Publishers Inc.

Garry, R.C. (1988).*Christian Counselling*: *A comprehensive Guide*. Dallas: Word Publishing.

Geisler, N.L. and Feinberg P.D. (1980). *Introduction to Philosophy*: A Christian Perspective. Grand Rapids, Michigan: Baker Book House.

Gelles, R.J. (2009). "*Child Abuse*" Microsoft Encarta (DVD).

Harrison, E.F. and Others, eds, (1960) *Wycliffe Dictionary of Theology*. Grand Rapids, Michigan: Baker Book House.

Hesselgrave, D.J. (1991).*Communicating Christ Cross-Culturally*. Grand Rapids, Michigan: Zondervan Publishing House.

Isiramen, C and Akhilomen, D. (1988). *Understanding Essays in Philosophy of Religion, Ethics and Early Church Controversies*. Lagos: AB Associates Publishers.

Janvier, G. and Thaba, B. (1997). *Leadership*: *An African*. Kaduna: Baraka Press and Publishers the Ltd.

Johnson, D. and Vanvonderen J.(1991). The *Subtle Power of Spiritual Abuse*. Minneapolis, Minnesota: Bethany House Publishers.

Kane, J.H.(1982). *A Concise History of Christian World Mission*. Grand Rapids, Michigan: Baker Book House.

Lakein, A.(2003). *How to Get Control of Your Time and Your Life*. Benin: SelfImprovement Publishing.

Martin, G.L. (1987). *Counselling for Family Violence and Abuse*. Waco, Texas: Word.

Montagu, A.(1965).*Life Before Birth*. New York: Signot Books.

Murphy J.M.(2000). *An International Ministers' Manual*. Arusha, Tanzania: Hundredfold Ministries Int'l.

Mullins, E.Y.(1917). *The Christian Religion in Its Doctrinal Expression*. Nashville: S.S.B. of south Baptist Convention.

Myers, B.L. (1999).*Walking With the* Poor: *Principles and Practice of Transformational Development*. Mary Knoll, New York: Obis Books

Ndukwe, S. O. (1998). *God's Eternal Purpose and Plan in the Ages* .Aba: Assemblies of God Press.

Newman, B. (1997).*Ten Laws of Leadership*. Benin: Marvellous Christian Publishers.

Noyce, G.(1988).*Pastoral Ethics: Professional Responsibilities of the Clergy*. Nashville: Abindon.

Okereke, C. C. (2012). *Lectures in Religious Ethics*. Enugu: Esodev Ltd.

Okeiyi, J.C. (2012) *Sexual Purity*. Lagos: Soteria Publishing House.

Onimhawo,J.A. (1998).*Euthanasia and African Culture*. Ibadan: Stirling-Horden Publishers (Nig. O Ltd.

Peale, N.V. (1986).*Why Some Positive Thinkers Get powerful Results*. New York: Oliver Nelson Publishers.

Pearlman, M. (1937).*Knowing the Doctrines of the Bible*. Springfield, Missouri: Gospel Publishing House.

Ramm, B. (1970).*Protestant Biblical Interpretation*. Grand Rapids, Michigan: Baker Book House.

Speer, E.R. (1990). *Christianity and the Nations*. New York: Revel.

Trull, J.E. and Carter, J.C. (1984).*Ministerial Ethics, 2nd Edition*. Grand Rapids, Michigan: Baker Academics.

Wemp, C. S. and Robert, H.C.(2007).*The Guide to Practical, Dynamic and Effective Pastoring*. Oshodi, Lagos: African Pastors Literature Trust.

Wilmington, D.H. (1984). *Wilmington's Guide to the Bible*. Wheaton, Illinois: Publishers Inc.

Zimmerman, T. F. and Others, eds. (1995). *And He Gave Pastors: Pastoral Theology in Action*. Springfield, Missouri: Gospel Publishing House.